The **TRUTH** about Yellow Pages

Making Them Work for You

The **TRUTH** about Yellow Pages

Making Them Work for You

Tom Davis

St. Lucie Press
Delray Beach, Florida

Copyright ©1997 by St. Lucie Press

All rights reserved. No part of this publication may be reproduced, stored in a retrieval system or transmitted in any form or by any means, electronic, mechanical, photocopying, recording or otherwise, without the prior written permission of the publisher.

Printed and bound in the U.S.A. Printed on acid-free paper.
10 9 8 7 6 5 4 3 2 1

ISBN 1-57444-078-0

All rights reserved. Authorization to photocopy items for internal or personal use, or the personal or internal use of specific clients, is granted by St. Lucie Press, provided that $.50 per page photocopied is paid directly to Copyright Clearance Center, 222 Rosewood Drive, Danvers, MA 01923 USA. The fee code for users of the Transactional Reporting Service is ISBN 1-57444-078-0 1/97/$100/$.50. The fee is subject to change without notice. For organizations that have been granted a photocopy license by the CCC, a separate system of payment has been arranged.

The copyright owner's consent does not extend to copying for general distribution, for promotion, for creating new works, or for resale. Specific permission must be obtained from St. Lucie Press for such copying.

Direct all inquiries to St. Lucie Press, Inc., 100 E. Linton Blvd., Suite 403B, Delray Beach, Florida 33483.

Phone: (561) 274-9906
Fax: (561) 274-9927

S$_L^t$

Published by
St. Lucie Press
100 E. Linton Blvd., Suite 403B
Delray Beach, FL 33483

TABLE OF CONTENTS

About the Author vii

Introduction 1

1 A Mirror of a Market 7

2 Usage Drives the Yellow Pages 17

3 The Exception, Not the Rule 25

4 The Domination Principle 33

5 A Tale of Four Businesses 47

6 Buying Strategies 53
  Step-Up 66
  Early Close Incentives 67
  Buy One, Get One 68
  Additional Directory Discounts 69
  Free Coupons 69
  Sample Marketing Plans 71

7 Ad Design to Get Attention 79

8 Copy: Hitting Them Between the Eyes! 89

9 Putting Your Ad Together 97

10 The Sales Representative: Friend or Foe? 103

11 Making the Advertising Work 109

12 Tying It All Together 117

13 The Past, The Present, The Future 123

14 Dispelling the Myths 131

ABOUT THE AUTHOR

Tom Davis has over 30 years experience in the Yellow Pages industry. As President of Better Business Builders, Inc. of Maitland, Florida, he has brought the seller's expertise to the buyer through consultant services and workshops for buyers of Yellow Pages advertising. He retired in 1994 from a long relationship with the Reuben H. Donnelley Corporation. His current clients include the Disney Corporation, franchises such as Purofirst International, Inc. and Truly Nolan Pest Control, and major names in the telecommunications industry such as BellSouth.

INTRODUCTION

It is said that all good things come to those who wait. In the case of this book, I believe this is so. I originally wrote the book over three years before I found a publisher for it. In the process of waiting, I had some new experiences that caused me to rewrite much of the book.

For over twenty-seven years, I was involved in the selling of Yellow Pages advertising. After twenty years in the business, I started thinking about writing a book on the subject. I realized that few people work as hard as I did to truly understand this very debatable product. Most people involved in selling Yellow Pages advertising are far more concerned with how much they can sell than understanding how and why their product works and how they can use it to truly benefit their customers.

A few years after I came to this realization, I started writing the book. At that time and during the period I was completing the book, I came from a salesman's perspective. I looked at the book as a vehicle for telling the positive side of the Yellow Pages. To a great extent, I now realize that I originally wrote the book with a chip on my shoulder. It was my chance to tell all the people who didn't listen to me when I was selling the product how good it can be and how they can benefit from it. In hindsight, my motives were good but my perspective was skewed.

In 1994, I took early retirement from the Reuben H. Donnelley Corporation and started a new career as a consultant, with the mission of helping in the buying of Yellow Pages advertising. At this time, I completed the book and embarked upon the adventure of trying to find a publisher interested in what I had to say on the subject. What a sobering experience! It is far easier to write a book than it is to find someone to publish it. If you can't stand rejection, I suggest you never consider writing a book. There is enough rejection in the process to more than fill a lifetime.

It became evident that I was not going to quickly earn any money in the form of book royalties, and so I started my consulting practice in earnest. As a consultant, I evaluate my clients' potential in Yellow Pages advertising and develop strategies for them in terms of budget, directories, ad size, layout, content, etc. In fulfilling this role, I come between the sales representatives and my clients. I become the buyer. In doing so, I am able to see the process of buying Yellow Pages advertising from an entirely different perspective.

As I helped advertisers in markets that were new to me, I found myself needing to rely upon the input of the various sales representatives serving those markets. I heard conflicting claims from competitive directories. I encountered sales representatives who had almost no customer orientation. Frequently there was lack of follow-up. Promises were not kept, and mistakes were frequently made. I began to understand what it is like to be a Yellow Pages customer and why so many advertisers have such great resistance to the entire process.

Like all sales organizations, the Yellow Pages industry has its good sales representatives and its bad ones. Some really know what they are doing and others barely do. Some are helpful and some get in the way. Many are not nearly as good as the products they represent. In other cases, very fine ones represent products of inferior value, which is a shame. In fact, when I believed that was the case, I suggested they consider selling for their far superior competitor.

As I went through these new experiences, I kept thinking about how I had presented my thoughts in the book as it was written at the time. Over time, it became obvious to me that if I were going to write the book to the best of my ability, it needed a major overhaul. I understood the buyer better and had to write the book in a way that demonstrated that understanding. I hope you sense that understanding in this *new and revised* version.

My purpose is the same as it was originally. I want to help you develop a more complete understanding of a product most buyers believe they understand far more than they truly do. A very dear, departed friend said to me many times, "The secret to making money is buying, not selling." How right he was!

As I look back, I realize that I made so much more money through the years for my customers than I ever made for myself. In fact, I made much more for my customers than I made for my company. As you explore this work, I think you will see more clearly why I say this and why it is so.

One of the problems with buying Yellow Pages advertising is most buyers have very strong opinions about its relative worth to their business or professional practice. Far more underestimate rather than overestimate its potential. Because this is true, if you are a buyer, or prospective buyer, I ask you to try to set those opinions aside and open your mind to the possibility that there is more gold in the Yellow Pages than you may realize. And relax! I am going to agree with some of your thoughts. In fact, in some cases, you may be completely right. But the truth is few people are truly experts on the subject. There are things you can learn about this product—things that will benefit you if you act upon your newly acquired understanding.

Like most authors, there are many people I have to thank for their assistance in helping me produce my final product. First, I thank the Reuben H. Donnelley Corporation. They hired me in 1966. They gave me excellent sales training. They put me in various positions in their Training Department over the years which resulted in developing my teaching and writing skills. Their policy of account continuity enabled me to serve the same basic customers for many years. This gave me a much better understanding of the product I was selling than I ever would have achieved if I had not been able to build the customer relationships I did through the years. And, finally, they offered an early retirement package that gave me the resources to do what I had wanted to do for quite a few years: consult and educate!

Even more important in the final analysis were the customers I served and tried to serve over the years. Those I tried to serve but was unable to taught me things only they could teach me. They taught me the importance of negative opinions of Yellow Pages advertising in the production of poor results from the advertising. They taught me that many more buyers are concerned with the "cost" of advertising than they are with the potential income from it. They taught me that far more business owners hold their businesses back for various reasons than take their businesses as far as they could potentially go. They taught me that most business owners and professionals are more concerned with just making a living than building a highly successful business or practice.

The preceding statements may sound a little harsh, but I am not making value judgments here. Who am I to say how successful someone should want to be? Everyone has the right to do what they believe is in their best interest. What I am saying is there are great differences between the opinions of individuals in the same markets and the same businesses or professions when it comes to the relative value of Yellow Pages advertising. Those differences of opinion result in different actions. Those different actions produce different results. There is something to learn from all of the opinions, actions, and results. All of them contributed to my increased understanding of this product that is so highly debated.

Most of all, I want to thank the relatively small percentage of customers who had the courage and foresight to truly test the Yellow Pages to its limits. Without them, I could never have learned how good the product truly can be. I also learned that few of them ever really test the product as far as they could. As a result, it was a relatively small percentage of this group who gave me my greatest education in terms of producing maximum results from the Yellow Pages.

I thank St. Lucie Press for believing in the book and putting their knowledge of the publishing business and their money behind it. Many times, I considered self-publishing the book. I knew I could sell enough copies to make a profit, but I am also realistic enough to recognize that my ability to distribute the book nationally is limited and that only a good publisher could get this book in as many hands as possible.

Since the book has now landed in your hands, I want to thank you for spending your money and your time to let me tell my story to you. You are the reason I have written this book. May you benefit from your efforts many times over!

And now, *The Truth About Yellow Pages.*

1 A MIRROR OF A MARKET

Just what is the Yellow Pages? There are many ways to describe it. It is a classified directory. It is a directional medium. It is a point-of-purchase medium. It is a great source of business for some, one of many places to advertise for others, and a medium of little to no importance for others. Many people use it like a bible, others use it occasionally, and still others almost never use it for their buying needs. I call it "a mirror of a market."

All advertising mediums mirror their audiences. Advertisers buy according to audience size and type. For example, different radio stations in the same market are attractive to different businesses based upon the type of audience they have. Each station appeals to certain segments of a market. A station's advertiser base will generally indicate the audience it reaches. The same applies to magazines and television stations.

Newspapers also mirror their audiences (readership). Businesses that advertise in the sports section generally do not advertise in the front page section and vice versa. Department stores buy half-page and full-page ads because the ads produce a lot of sales for them and have proven to be profitable. Employment agencies generally buy small ads in the classified section because that is what works best for them.

Yet no advertising medium mirrors a specific geographical market to the extent and with the detail the Yellow Pages does. After all, Yellow Pages is essentially an information medium and as such contains information needed by buyers in the market it covers. In fact, a directory that fails to adequately give this detailed information to its users will lose usage and frequently fail.

One way a directory mirrors a market is by the size of the directory. The size of a directory is an indication of the size of the population it covers rather than the geographical size of its market. Some rural directories cover larger geographical areas than many metropolitan directories, but this is not reflected in the relative size of the directories. In fact, the reverse would be true. The directory that serves the larger population would be larger than the directory that covers the larger geographical area.

The smallest directories contain two columns per page. They are found in sparsely populated, rural areas or in what are termed neighborhood directories in metropolitan areas. Larger rural areas and other neighborhood-type directories contain three columns per page. The largest metropolitan areas generally have directories with four columns per page. A few metropolitan areas have found it necessary to go to five columns per page or to split their directories into two alphabetical editions, such as A through L and M through Z.

These differences in size tell you the differences in the total dollar potential of directories. Two-column directories do not produce hundreds of thousands of dollars of business for a single advertiser. Very large metropolitan directories can produce that volume of income and more for many of their advertisers.

The size of a directory is also a good indication of the cost of its ads. In the smallest directories, you may be able to purchase a quarter-page ad for as little as $40 per month. In some of the largest directories, quarter-page ads can cost $1,000 per month and more. There is a direct correlation between the size of a directory and the cost of an ad, just as there is a direct correlation between the size of a directory and the total amount of income it can produce for its advertisers.

The size of a directory can also reflect the quality of a market. As a general rule, a directory that covers a higher quality market will contain more pages than a directory that serves a comparable population base with lesser economic strength. A better quality market will usually have more businesses serving it. Yellow Pages directories that serve higher quality markets will have headings that are more competitive in terms of the number and size of ads.

Sometimes the difference in directory size in similar population areas is a reflection of the quality of the Yellow Pages sales organization selling the directory. All sales organizations are not created equal. The best ones sell a higher percentage of their potential advertiser base and sell larger ads as well.

Changes in the size of a directory over a period of years reflect the growth, lack of growth, or decline in the population of the area covered by the directory. While this correlation may be obvious, other factors can also affect the size of a directory over time. In recent years, many Yellow Pages publishers have introduced buying incentive plans. Prior to the introduction of such plans, all ads of the same size in the same directory cost the same. That is frequently no longer the case. Many publishers now discount ads for a variety of reasons. Therefore, they increase the space purchased or prevent the loss of space purchased within a directory through the use of such plans. By discounting space, publishers experience less income per page but are able to mask to some degree what is really going on within their product, although this is not the intention of such buying incentive plans; they are intended as selling tools. As you will learn later in this book, incentive plans can be quite beneficial to buyers of Yellow Pages advertising.

The size of a directory can also reflect the Yellow Pages competitive situation within a market. Today, many markets are served by two or more directories. Independent, non-telephone-company publishers as well as telephone companies from outside a market are now competing with the local telephone company. What had been a monopolistic situation has turned into a dog-eat-dog competitive situation all over the country. This is the greatest reason for the introduction of buying incentive plans.

The size of competing directories within a market can reflect the market share of each directory. If two directories cover the same geographical area and one has twice as much advertising as its competitor, the larger directory has penetrated the advertiser base much more effectively. Over time, this will provide a good indication of the relative usage of the directories. The size of a directory is ultimately driven by its usage. If usage declines, a decline in advertiser support will follow. If usage increases, it becomes easier for the publisher to sell more space.

The more directories that serve a market, the more difficult it is for any of them to increase in size. A new publisher in a market will do almost anything to grow or to at least not shrink in size. A directory that loses space at a faster rate than it can replace it with new space is an indication that advertisers are not happy with the results from their ads. In the directory business, this is the kiss of death. There are only so many businesses in a market. Once they have lost faith in a directory, the publisher may never regain their confidence or their business.

If you are in one of these competitive markets, it is important that you understand exactly what you see when you compare the directories. Sometimes the largest directory may not be the best buy. Some directories have been designed to cover the distribution areas of two or more of their competitors' directories. This is a common approach when some publishers enter a new market. Since they have a larger potential advertiser base than each of the directories they overlap, they frequently can produce a larger directory. This does not mean it is a better buy for anyone. The users of the directories will decide the success of this strategy in the long run.

The competitive directory situation in a market is one of the most confusing aspects of buying Yellow Pages advertising. There is much to study in the various directories to determine just what they are telling you about themselves. This subject will be revisited in Chapter 6—Buying Strategies.

Size is the "big picture" of a directory. The fine points are found inside the directory. The number of headings that are published and the amount of advertising under specific headings can tell you a lot about the market covered by the directory. Essentially, the same headings are available in the vast majority of directories. Headings such as AUTOMOBILE REPAIRING & SERVICE, CATERERS, LOCKS & LOCKSMITHS, RESTAURANTS, and SIGNS appear in virtually every directory across the country. In contrast, while the heading CASINOS may be available in every directory, it can only be found in select areas, such as Atlantic City and Las Vegas. The same is true for the heading EXPORTERS. It does not appear in most directories, yet the Miami directory has over forty pages under that heading.

The more headings that appear in a given directory, the more diverse the market it covers. Larger directories will have literally hundreds of headings that do not appear in smaller directories. Many of the headings will be for wholesalers and manufacturers. This simply reflects the wider variety of businesses that exist in more populated areas. The larger the population base, the greater the variety of businesses serving that base.

The number and size of ads under a specific heading also say a great deal about a market. In northern directories, the heading HEATING CONTRACTORS will have more ads and larger ads than the AIR CONDITIONING CONTRACTORS & SYSTEMS heading will contain, The reverse will be true in directories in the deep South. Another example would be the Orlando, Florida directories. They have pages and pages of ads listed under HOTELS and MOTELS because of the large concentration of hotels and motels in that large tourist market.

The quality of a market for a particular product or service will frequently be reflected by the size of the ads appearing under its heading. Directories that cover markets with relatively high per capita income will usually have some large display ads under headings such as TRAVEL AGENCIES & BUREAUS, JEWELERS—RETAIL, and FUR BUSINESS—RETAIL. Directories that cover markets with a lot of new construction will usually have comparatively large ads under headings such as BUILDING MATERIALS, CONCRETE—READY-MIXED, and LUMBER—RETAIL.

A Yellow Pages directory also mirrors how good it is, or is not, as an advertising medium for specific types of businesses. As stated earlier, this is true to a great extent for all major advertising media: radio, television, newspapers, magazines, billboards, and direct mail. Not all of these advertising mediums are equal in value to a specific business. By studying who the major advertisers are in a medium, you can identify those businesses that profit the most from the use of that medium. This is definitely true of the Yellow Pages. Without a doubt, certain businesses profit more from advertising in it than others.

A significant number of display ads appearing under a specific heading is a clear indication there is a large amount of business flowing through the heading. This is one way the Yellow Pages tells you where to spend your money. The opposite is also true. With few exceptions, if you do not see many of your competitors currently spending their money for large display ads under a specific heading, you should think long and hard before you consider purchasing a large ad under that heading. If the opportunity to make a lot of money from the heading existed, chances are someone would have an aggressive ad under the heading.

Changes that occur over time under some headings mirror changes in demand for certain products and/or services. Twenty-five years ago, there were no headings starting with the word "computer." There was a heading for DATA PROCESSING EQUIPMENT & SUPPLIES, but essentially no one bought advertising under it. There were only a few manufacturers of such equipment at the time, and frankly they did not sell their equipment through buying advertising in the Yellow Pages. In the mid-1970s, the heading COMPUTERS—DEALERS was established, but little advertising appeared under it because there were not many dealers at that time. Computers were still bought directly from the manufacturers for the most part. The 1980s and 1990s have seen tremendous growth in advertising under COMPUTERS—DEALERS and other computer headings. This growth in advertising mirrored the growth that occurred in the computer industry over that time period.

Another example of the mirroring effect over time was the citizens band radio industry. Until the early to middle 1970s, very little advertising for this product appeared in the Yellow Pages because few people bought

CBs and few businesses sold them. As the demand for CBs increased, so did the amount of advertising in the Yellow Pages by this industry. What goes up eventually comes down, and that is what happened to the CB radio industry outside of and inside of the Yellow Pages. The market declined, the number of dealers declined, and the amount of money spent in the Yellow Pages by the industry declined.

The real puzzle about Yellow Pages advertising is how it reflects the wide variety of opinions of its advertisers in terms of its value as an advertising medium. For example, one plumbing contractor may believe it is worthwhile to buy a full-page ad, but some of his direct competitors don't buy as much as a bold type listing. Why is it that the majority of businesses under most headings do little advertising and only a minority of their competitors purchase ads of any size? There are some valid reasons for this diversity of representation and there are many reasons that really do not make any sense.

Yellow Pages advertising reflects anywhere from extensive knowledge to some knowledge to almost complete ignorance on the part of its advertisers. If this statement surprises you, it shouldn't. What training do most business owners have in buying any advertising, let alone Yellow Pages advertising? Very little, I assure you. Much of what they do know has been learned by trial and error, which is a difficult way to learn about anything. In terms of advertising, it is costly and time consuming.

What this means is no matter what your opinion may be about the Yellow Pages, you can always find reinforcement of that opinion in the directory. You can see whatever you want to see under your heading. You can find large advertisers who tell you Yellow Pages are very profitable, many more who say it has some value, and a great number who believe Yellow Pages to be of almost no value whatsoever. It is up to you to decide who is right.

One of the real traps in Yellow Pages advertising is putting too much trust in how large corporations treat it as a source of income. My consulting business specializes in working with medium-size to large corporations. I do so because I find they have the most difficult time buying Yellow Pages ads well. They have a tendency to ask the wrong questions as they make their decisions. They ask, "What is our policy?" without questioning the policy. They ask, "What representation do we need?" without asking, "How much profit can we potentially make from the Yellow Pages?" They oversimplify Yellow Pages and Yellow Pages usage and, as a result, frequently underbuy.

I am not singling out large companies. They are successful, so how can I criticize them? I simply realize that just because they are successful does not mean they are doing everything perfectly. Some major corporations do owe a great deal of their success to the Yellow Pages, but most do not. They have built their businesses through other methods of marketing their products and services. As you look at how major companies utilize the Yellow Pages, keep in mind that it is only one source of business. Even if they do not use Yellow Pages very effectively, there are still many other sources they can and do find profitable.

I have learned the strengths of Yellow Pages advertising from a relatively small percentage of the businesses I have contacted through the years. Most of the weaknesses, or perceived weaknesses, were pointed out to me over and over by the majority of Yellow Pages advertisers I have known. Those who make the most money from their ads reflect this attitude by purchasing the same or even more advertising year after year. That is the true test of the medium. If you are going to learn from other advertisers, learn from the larger advertisers. They understand the final mirroring aspect of Yellow Pages advertising: usage.

Larger advertisers understand that:

- Larger directories have more usage than smaller directories.
- Directories declining in size have declining usage.
- Directories growing in size have growing usage.
- Users are essentially potential customers.
- Successful ads appeal to as many users as possible.

- Yellow Pages advertising is a head-to-head competitive arena. How you represent yourself determines how you compete in this arena.

More than anything, the Yellow Pages reflects usage. This is a far more complex subject than most Yellow Pages advertisers consider it to be. Therefore, the next chapter is devoted to the subject of usage. For now, it is sufficient to note that a Yellow Pages directory tells you how often it is used, what products and services have the greatest demand from this usage, whether that usage is growing or declining over time, the relative dollar value of the usage, and the opinions of its advertisers concerning its usage.

As other main points are developed in the following chapters, you will be able to find the validity of these points reflected in ads in your local Yellow Pages directory. Not all ads will back up these points, but if you look hard enough, you will find good examples of local businesses successfully using these effective principles of Yellow Pages advertising. The directories you examine will mirror successful and unsuccessful uses of the medium. They will tell you the current level of knowledge of Yellow Pages advertising on the part of your competitors. This book will teach you how to improve your ability to read the "mirror" called Yellow Pages so you can use it more effectively.

2
USAGE DRIVES THE YELLOW PAGES

You know to what degree you use the Yellow Pages. You also know how you use the Yellow Pages. The problem is everyone doesn't use the Yellow Pages as frequently, or infrequently, as you do, nor do they use it exactly the same way you do. This chapter will open your eyes to the depth of the subject of Yellow Pages usage. The better you understand why and how the Yellow Pages is used by your prospective buyers, the better job you can do in making your advertising appeal to the buyers you are trying to attract.

Just as usage drives the Yellow Pages, usage is driven by demand—demand for particular products and/or services at particular times. The greater the demand for a particular product or service, the more likely there will be greater usage of the Yellow Pages headings devoted to that product or service. If the demand for a product or service has been and will be growing, the usage of Yellow Pages, generally speaking, will do likewise.

Yellow Pages usage is situational. If, why, when, and how you or anyone else uses the Yellow Pages is determined by the particular situation at the time that person decides to at least consider buying a product or service.

The "if" is determined by whether or not the buyer needs to refer to some source as an aid in the buying process. If a source is needed to provide the name, telephone number, address, or other information about the seller of a particular product or service, a Yellow Pages directory becomes a prospective source to be used.

The "why" involves the expectation of the prospective buyer that the Yellow Pages can provide the information being sought. Certain things are expected when someone refers to a Yellow Pages directory. The prospective buyer expects the directory to contain (or at least hopes it will contain) the information needed to go about the potential buying process. It is that expectation that causes the Yellow Pages to be chosen as a reference source.

The "when" is determined by how ready the buyer is to make the purchase. The majority of references to the Yellow Pages are followed by some sort of action: a phone call, a letter, or a visit on the part of the buyer. That is a fairly unique quality of Yellow Pages usage (similar to the classified section of the newspaper) because it involves action on the part of someone who is ready to buy. While not all Yellow Pages usage involves buying or results in a purchase, this is the usage we will focus upon in this book. It is the majority of the usage of a Yellow Pages directory and the reason advertisers are willing to invest money in this advertising medium in the first place.

The "how" is affected by Yellow Pages usage habits of the individual, familiarity with potential sources for the product, and, most of all, the particular situation of the user at the time of usage. When I discuss the subject of Yellow Pages usage with Yellow Pages advertisers, the conversation is quite simplistic at the beginning. Usually advertisers oversimplify their own usage. They make statements such as, "When I use the Yellow Pages I always...." When I bring up the subject of situations surrounding the usage, they start to realize that they do not always use Yellow Pages the same way. There are differences in the "if, why, when, and how" they use the Yellow Pages.

Think about your own usage of Yellow Pages. Think about how it is affected if you have bought the product before, bought it from the source you are considering now, bought it in the community in which you are located, and are not in a hurry to buy the particular product or service. When you have bought the product before from the business you are considering now in the community in which you are located and can wait if you have to for the product, there is a certain way you will go about using the Yellow Pages at that time. Change just one of the factors and your usage may change as well.

If you have not bought the product or service before, that change alone may have an effect on whom you will consider as a source of the product or service. If your usual source of similar products or services does not have or do what you need, your usage may also be affected. If your usual source is not located in or near the community in which you are located at the time, your usage may well be affected. Finally, if time is of the essence, you may well change who you will consider as a supplier of the product or service at that time.

The more you examine these differences, the more you will realize there is no one pattern of usage you always follow when you use the Yellow Pages. You may even discover there are some differences in your usage when you are buying for your personal needs as opposed to when you are buying for business and professional needs. If you have employees who buy for your business, ask yourself if you think they buy the same way for your business that they buy for their personal needs. You would probably agree that at least some of them are much more careful buyers for themselves than they are for you. The same is true for some of the buyers of products or services you sell to other businesses or professionals.

There are, therefore, different types of usage. Personal usage is the type most frequently considered as Yellow Pages usage. Another type of usage is business to business. If you doubt its existence, look at headings such as PRINTERS, OFFICE FURNITURE & EQUIPMENT—DEALERS, and COPYING MACHINES & SUPPLIES. They "mirror" the fact that this business-to-business type of usage exists.

A third type of usage is industrial. Like all buyers, industrial buyers prefer to do business locally if at all possible for obvious reasons of convenience. The Yellow Pages provides such buyers easy access to possible local sources of supply for various products and services. This type of usage is frequently much greater than many advertisers realize. It should not be overlooked by potential advertisers because of the size of many of the purchases that may be involved in an industrial use of the Yellow Pages.

Another frequently overlooked source of Yellow Pages usage is governments and governmental agencies. With the growth of all forms of government has come a comparable growth in their purchases. How does Yellow Pages come into this picture? First, Yellow Pages is a reliable source that can be used to build local bid lists. Second, not all government purchases are made through the bid process. Governments sometimes have needs that just do not fit with obtaining bids as part of the buying process. For example, when there is an emergency, governments may not have the luxury of time to solicit bids for a product or service.

It is important to understand the reasons behind Yellow Pages usage. It will help you to understand why the Yellow Pages is used as often as it is. More importantly, it will help you to better understand how you can capitalize on usage of the Yellow Pages and get a better return for your money from the ads you purchase.

I refer to Yellow Pages usage as "the process of elimination." As I explain this process, I would ask you again to measure it against your own usage of the Yellow Pages. You will probably find you use this process most of the time. The simplest example of this process is when someone knows exactly whom they are going to call when they refer to the Yellow Pages. In this example, everyone is eliminated from consideration except for the business or businesses knowingly being sought. Ads or listings for other businesses are of no interest or importance to this user. When more than one business is being sought, the usage of Yellow Pages usually results in the elimination of some businesses before the decision is made as to which businesses will be used to provide the product or service.

Now think about instances when you did not have a particular source in mind for a product or service. You knew what you wanted; you just didn't know who was going to supply it. In such situations, chances are you also used "the process of elimination." When you did, you were helped by some of the potential sources in this elimination process. Potential sources not represented in the directory in which you were looking or under the particular heading to which you were referring eliminated themselves. If you only referred to the first few listings at the beginning of the heading, all of the sources located elsewhere in the heading were eliminated as well. If you only referred to the display ads under the heading, sources without display ads were eliminated. They were eliminated because they did not have a display ad under that heading and because you chose to only look at display ads.

"The process of elimination" goes deeper. Advertisers are eliminated for a wide variety of reasons other than not being considered in the first place. As you read an ad, information it contains or fails to contain assists you in this process. The strongest factor is the physical location of the business or practice. No one factor has as much of an impact on the elimination process than the location factor. This is especially true when you are going to travel to the location. When you are looking for potential sources in a particular town or a nearby town, you will usually eliminate from consideration any source located outside of those communities. When we discuss developing the content of your ad later in this book, you will see just how important this factor is.

Hours of operation can also be an elimination factor. When you need to find a business that is open on Saturday, you will probably eliminate all advertisers that indicate they are open Monday through Friday from nine to five. If you need a source that is open twenty-four hours a day, you will probably eliminate the majority of ads you read.

As we explore "the process of elimination" throughout this book, you will see that it answers many of the questions and concerns about Yellow Pages advertising and its effectiveness. This elimination process ranges far and wide. When a Yellow Pages user chooses to use one directory over another directory, that user has eliminated all of the ads in the directory(ies) excluded. When an advertiser chooses to advertise in one directory and does not advertise in other competitive directory(ies), another form of "the process of elimination" occurs. The elimination is done not by the user but by the advertiser. The advertiser is saying, "I want to exclude that usage as a potential source of business or clients." That is not how an advertiser normally states it, but that is really what the advertiser is saying when a particular directory is not utilized as an advertising medium.

Advertisers use this process even in directories in which they advertise. Frequently an advertiser has to consider more than one heading in a given directory. In some businesses, there may be dozens of headings that could potentially be considered. For every heading that is overlooked or ignored by the advertiser, its users are eliminated as potential customers or clients. In most cases, the usage of one heading within a directory has nothing to do with the usage of a totally different heading. A printer with a half-page ad under the heading PRINTERS will not benefit from that ad when someone refers to the heading COPYING SERVICE. This is why I do not recommend buying a listing under a heading such as COPYING SERVICE and adding a line of copy at the bottom of the ad that says, "See Our Ad Under Printers." This is frequently done in the Yellow Pages. What it fails to recognize is that users refer to the heading COPYING SERVICE for a reason and probably make their choices of potential suppliers from that heading. An advertiser who understands this element of usage would change the line of copy to say something like, "Fast Turnaround—Very Competitive Prices."

Usage creates two reasons for considering advertising in the Yellow Pages—offense and defense. The offense side considers the fact that Yellow Pages users frequently use the Yellow Pages as an aid in determining where to buy. These users potentially can become anyone's customers. They are the newcomers, the first-time buyers, and the buyers whose previous suppliers went out of business. Although this is the most obvious side of Yellow Pages advertising, it still is not fully understood by all advertisers, as reflected in the way various advertisers compete for this usage. Some are very aggressive with their representation, but most are not, and some do not even appear. The usage is there, but recognition of the importance of the usage differs, frequently dramatically.

The defense side is recognized by many advertisers but in what I consider to be a negative way. One of the most common descriptions of Yellow Pages advertising by its advertisers is, "It's a necessary evil." In other words, "I know I have to be there, but I don't like it, and I am not going to be there more than I think I absolutely have to." These words are sweet to the ears of the advertiser who really understands Yellow Pages usage. These words result in underrepresentation on the part of advertisers with this negative perspective, which means less competition and weaker competition for the advertiser who understands the defensive side of Yellow Pages.

Early in my career, I was on an interview in which a Yellow Pages advertiser was giving a testimonial to the local publisher about the effectiveness of his Yellow Pages advertising. When asked about the business it generated, he said, "It's not the business I get that concerns me most. It is the business I wouldn't get if I wasn't there." These were the words of a very successful businessman who understood that business could be taken from him if he let a competitor steal it. He recognized that many users who came to the Yellow Pages intending to do business with him could be stolen away by another competitor's ad if he underrepresented his company.

To understand how all of this applies to you, stop and think about your potential customers or clients. You know what products or services they need. That is why you offer them. You know what kind of buying situations they encounter. You know whether or not they seek out a different supplier in an emergency situation. You know whether or not your market and potential customer base are growing with new, unfamiliar buyers. You know why people buy your product or service and why they do not. The more aware you are of if, when, why, and how your potential customers or clients use the Yellow Pages, the more intelligent buyer you will become. The average business owner does not give usage the kind of consideration it deserves. The more consideration you give it, the easier it will be for you to compete effectively in this oversimplified, greatly misunderstood advertising medium.

3 THE EXCEPTION, NOT THE RULE

If you are truly going to understand the Yellow Pages, you must understand its limitations as well as its strengths. It is rare that a majority of customers for any product or service would use the Yellow Pages as a buying source for that product or service. Certainly businesses such as movers, taxis, and florists can derive a good percentage of their business from the Yellow Pages (although many owners of moving companies, cab companies, and flower shops would disagree with that statement). The truth is Yellow Pages advertising is not always used as a reference every time you or I need to buy something, which is why I call it "the exception, not the rule."

To expect that the majority of your potential customers will use the Yellow Pages when they need your products or services is expecting too much. What you do have a right to expect is enough usage to give you a return on your investment. That does not necessarily mean it will or can double your business. It does not mean that if your use Yellow Pages advertising profitably, your business will not fail. It does not mean that it even has to be your most important source of business.

Most buyers of Yellow Pages advertising have unreasonable expectations of what it should produce. Yellow Pages advertising can be a potent source of customers or clients for many kinds of businesses and professions. At the same time, there are many successful people in those businesses and professions who do not use Yellow Pages as even a minor source of income. Attorneys spend more money in Yellow Pages than any other single group, yet there is more income earned by the legal profession that does not come from Yellow Pages than comes from Yellow Pages. Thus, even in the legal profession, the Yellow Pages is the exception, not the rule.

A thought process used by many Yellow Pages advertisers and potential advertisers is as follows: "Most of my potential customers don't use the Yellow Pages; therefore, it is not a profitable place for me to advertise." Or "I get most of my business from...therefore, the Yellow Pages is not important to me." Or "I would never use the Yellow Pages to find a restaurant; therefore, people don't use the Yellow Pages to find restaurants." Or "Several of my larger competitors don't utilize Yellow Pages advertising; therefore, it must not work very well for my kind of business."

The first part of each of these statements may be totally true, but the conclusions drawn from them may be just as false. There are businesses that should not advertise in the Yellow Pages, and there are many that should not spend much of their advertising budgets in the Yellow Pages. But I have heard these statements from people in even the best of Yellow Pages businesses. I have heard these statements from owners of cab companies, casualty insurance agencies, florists, plumbers, automobile dealers, and even personal injury attorneys. Each believed his or her logic was correct and therefore Yellow Pages was of little consequence to him or her.

Returning to the "mirror of a market" explanation of Yellow Pages in Chapter 1, there are certain headings in Yellow Pages directories that do produce a considerable amount of income for their advertisers. Others are not as productive, and still others may be worth very little in terms of an investment for their advertisers. Generally speaking, the directory will tell you how good it is or is not for you as an investment. The question is how good is good and how good does it have to be.

As mentioned earlier, all Yellow Pages advertising has to do is be profitable for an advertiser. For most advertisers, if the advertising is profitable this year, the real profit from the advertising will come in future years. Most businesses get some degree of repeat business from their customers and clients. They usually get some degree of referral or "word-of-mouth" business as well. This is what I call "the snowball effect." It is the way advertisers can help build their business over time with the help of their Yellow Pages efforts. That is how most businesses are built. They have a constant influx of new customers, which results in an increase in their customer base, which refers additional new customers who become a part of the customer base.

This repeat aspect of Yellow Pages is more valuable for some than others. Businesses that rely on tourists may not generate a significant amount of repeat business, but they still may get significant word-of-mouth results. Infrequent types of purchases such as real estate, swimming pools, and even a personal injury case can also have limited repeat potential, but the potential still exists for word-of-mouth generation of customers.

One of the most obvious types of repeat business using Yellow Pages advertising is the automobile insurance business. That is the reason for the amount of advertising done by auto insurance agencies under the heading INSURANCE. Headings such as PEST CONTROL and PRINTERS are other examples. When this type of repeat potential exists, an advertiser with reasonable expectations will be satisfied with some profit the first year, knowing the real profit will come in the following years. It takes time to build a business, and it takes time for Yellow Pages advertising to produce its total return on the investment.

Where Yellow Pages is closer to the rule than the exception, you will see advertisers actively competing for the business being generated. It is safe to say that Yellow Pages advertising produces significant market share for the florist business, plumbing service companies, pest control companies, taxi companies, and movers. The headings devoted to these kinds of businesses are examples of the rule rather than the exception.

Some significant headings are exceptions as well. There is usually a significant amount of advertising under the heading AUTOMOBILE DEALERS—NEW CARS. The main reason for this is the total dollar value of the market. Even if Yellow Pages is only used by 10% of the market (and studies indicate usage is greater than 10%), that represents a significant amount of money flowing through this heading.

Automobile dealers as a group are interesting in terms of their opinions of Yellow Pages advertising. They know it is not the most important form of advertising available. They know they must spend large amounts of money in other media to be successful. They know they must make substantial investments in facilities and staff, as well as cars and parts inventories. Most of them fail to address the true nature of Yellow Pages as it involves their business. There is no one reason why someone would refer to the heading AUTOMOBILE DEALERS—NEW CARS. Reasons include inquiries about new cars or trucks, used cars or trucks, repairs, maintenance, parts, and renting or leasing. It is not that every potential customer uses the Yellow Pages to become a customer. It is just that the market is so huge and the ways of making money from the market so diverse that, in truth, the Yellow Pages can be an irreplaceable source of business for automobile dealers. It is the exception, not the rule, but an exception that cannot be derived from any other source. Business that results from references to the Yellow Pages can only be derived by those who try to get the references.

Another example of an exception is the heading RESTAURANTS. Restaurant owners, in my experience, have just as difficult a time buying Yellow Pages advertising as automobile dealers. I am not talking about owners of hot dog stands, sandwich shops, or fast-food franchises. I am talking about the kind of restaurant where the customer spends a significant amount of money for a meal. If you are not in the restaurant business, you probably believe that people use the Yellow Pages to find such restaurants. Yet many owners of such restaurants have trouble believing this usage exists. All advertisers have a potential problem in terms of their thinking about the Yellow Pages. The problem is they know too much about their business, their competition, and why they would not use the Yellow Pages to find their kind of business. They don't need to! They know who has what and does what and how well they do it. Frequently their potential customers do not.

Owners of Oriental restaurants seem to have a better understanding of Yellow Pages advertising. Certainly there is an aspect of their business that makes them more aware of Yellow Pages results than most restaurant owners. Many Oriental restaurants derive a significant amount of their business from carry-out orders that come in over the telephone. This probably has a lot to do with their seemingly increased awareness. Yet I have seen a large restaurant chain get into the carry-out business without showing much understanding of the value of Yellow Pages advertising to influence the volume of calls for carry-out orders. The amount of carry-out business generated probably came from almost any source imaginable other than Yellow Pages. The "exception" has always been there for them. They just have not realized it.

I am not singling out automobile dealers and restaurant owners. What I am saying applies to most advertisers who could use Yellow Pages as a source of revenue better than they currently do. Just as with usage, the thinking of most advertisers about the potential of Yellow Pages is too simplistic. Statements like, "It's not important to us" hide the fact that it frequently can have some importance. The fact that the majority of someone's business may come from other sources does not mean there is no money to be made from the Yellow Pages.

Yellow Pages advertising should be positioned exactly the same way as other potential revenue sources. Generally speaking, sales representatives will continuously produce sales for you that you could not get from any other source. Each marketing method has its own ability to produce income for those who use it effectively. Too often, a decision is made to stop using one advertising medium or method of marketing and replace it with another medium or method of marketing. If the medium or method being discarded has been unprofitable, that is one thing. What frequently happens, however, is a medium or method that has produced profitable results is discarded for another medium or method in hopes the new one will be more profitable. What is wrong with using both? If the one medium or method has been profitable and the one being considered will also be profitable, isn't the business better off with both? In most cases, the answer is yes. There are times when growth may not be desired, but for the majority of advertisers I worked with over the years, there was both room for and a desire for growth.

As you will learn throughout this book, I believe strongly in making one decision at a time when it comes to income-producing choices. I have often challenged a group of advertisers to think about the checks they write every month. I ask them to think about them one by one and isolate those checks they write every month that go to someone or something that produces revenue for them. What they realize is that very few of the checks fall into this category. Shouldn't they be the most important checks a business sends out every month? Wouldn't most businesses be better off if they had even more profitable sources to write checks to every month? Isn't that the life blood of most businesses and professional practices?

How does all of this apply to the exception, not the rule? Generally speaking, most businesses and professions derive the majority of their income from one or two major sources. This means that every other source or potential source falls into the exception category. Yet exception categories can contribute significantly to profits when used along with the major contributors to income. This brings us to the "occupancy theory of business."

Certain businesses are definitely occupancy-type businesses. The most obvious one is the hotel/motel industry. Owners of such businesses live and die by occupancy percentage. It is their break-even point! They know they must rent a certain number of rooms to be profitable. They know that this number of rooms is a certain percentage of the total number of rooms they have available over the period being evaluated. They also know that their profitability increases geometrically as they increase their occupancy rate. They know that once they reach the percentage they need to be in the black, each additional room they rent over that number is almost all profit. They have recovered their fixed costs, and their variable costs are a very small percentage of the total costs. Therefore, there is much profit in each room rented over and above the number required to be profitable.

There are other obvious occupancy-type businesses as well. Certainly restaurants, airlines, taxi companies, and movie theaters are also occupancy businesses. What about doctors, lawyers, consultants, and other similar fee-based businesses and professionals? Is a plumbing contractor an occupancy business? How about an automobile repair business? Many businesses are actually occupancy businesses but do not view themselves as such. When owners of such businesses consider the occupancy factor, they discover something of great potential value.

Do most owners of florist shops consider themselves to be in an occupancy business? I think not. Yet they pay floral arrangers to be there whether they are working constantly on arrangements one after another or they are waiting for the next order to be placed so they have something to do. Any business that has production employees of one type or another who are paid to be there whether they are working or not is, in my opinion, an occupancy business. This means that those businesses can profit considerably from some of the exception sources of income available to them. They do not have to double their size to double their profitability. All they have to do is increase the occupancy percentage of the occupancy parts of their business.

Consider the occupancy theory as it relates to your own business—not just in terms of Yellow Pages advertising, but in terms of increasing the profitability of your business or practice. As you think about your business or professional practice, revisit Yellow Pages advertising to determine how great the "exception" may be for you. Chances are you have underestimated its potential and can use it to gain more than you thought.

4

THE DOMINATION PRINCIPLE

In many ways, this is the most important chapter in this book. The more you believe the information presented in this chapter, the more you will do what will be most beneficial for you with your Yellow Pages advertising. Hopefully, you will understand the logic in what I call "the domination principle."

The domination principle applies to all advertising and marketing endeavors. It simply states that you will never get maximum results from any marketing or advertising effort unless you do it in a dominant way. Although this point may seem rather obvious, the truth is most businesses are never dominant in any form of marketing or advertising they use. One reason is not all businesses want the volume of business they would create for themselves by being dominant in their efforts. More frequently, the concern is the amount of money it would require to be dominant.

Let's start with the location of a business as a marketing tool. Some businesses are more location oriented than others. Certainly the fast-food industry falls into this category. You find the McDonald's, Burger Kings, and Wendy's of the world paying high prices for high-visibility locations. You don't find them on small side streets where it is difficult for customers to find them. It costs more money for such locations, but the success of such businesses proves the importance of the high-visibility location.

Next let's look at the use of sales representatives. If you have one salesman and a competitor has ten, which sales force do you think will sell the most? Which one will cost the most? How many large companies in truly competitive direct-selling industries have a small sales force? The answers are obvious, aren't they?

Now let's start to look at forms of advertising as a test of the domination principle. How many truly large companies doing business with the public rely strictly on word-of-mouth advertising? How many can you think of that are not a dominant advertiser in at least one advertising medium? For purposes of illustration, I will continue to use the fast-food industry as an example because there are a lot of points about how it gets its business that apply to the domination principle.

Certainly the fast-food chains such as McDonald's, Burger King, and Wendy's do more than merely buy expensive locations. While they do not use every form of advertising available to them, as a general rule they are relatively dominant in the use of the mediums they do utilize. The most obvious medium for them is television. They are among the list of dominant users of television advertising in terms of the amount of time they buy and the cost of their time slots. Notice that their smaller competitors do not advertise as strongly on television as "the big three." Is there a correlation?

Television advertising is very similar to radio advertising. You dominate it by being dominant on one station. You dominate it even more by being dominant on more than one station. Generally speaking, if you are going to run ten spots per day, you are better off directing all ten toward the same audience on one station than you are running one spot per day on each of ten stations. Better yet, you will produce even more for your business if you run ten spots per day on two, three, or more stations.

Consider the following story about a business I saw grow from one location to dozens of locations over a period of ten years. It is a wonderful example of the domination principle. It involves a local tire company that opened its first location and entered the highly competitive tire replacement business. The store had at least six tire chains to compete with when it opened its doors. I believe the key to the company's success was that the owner understood the domination principle, whether or not he called it that.

Certainly there were many forms of advertising the owner could have considered. The problem was that because he was in a metropolitan area, all of the major mediums (radio, television, newspaper, billboards, and Yellow Pages) were relatively expensive for a single-location start-up business. For rather obvious reasons, he chose the newspaper—specifically, the sports section of the local daily newspaper. This was a logical choice because most of his competitors advertised there as well.

How could a one-location business be a dominant player in a daily metropolitan newspaper? As mentioned earlier, he certainly wasn't the only tire business advertising in the sports section. Some of his competitors bought quarter-page and even half-page ads. How could he be dominant? He did so by being the only tire business to run an ad in the sports section every day. His ad was about one inch by two columns. It was loaded with prices of various sizes and brands of tires. He left just enough room in the ad for his name, address, telephone number, and credit cards accepted.

While he didn't spend as much money in newspaper advertising as his bigger competitors, he was there every day. He apparently decided he could dominate with frequency since he couldn't dominate with size. The ads must have worked because he soon opened another location. When he did, his newspaper ad got slightly larger so that he could add another address and telephone number. Eventually, he grew to three locations, then four locations, etc.

After he had established multiple locations, he started advertising on television and radio. He quickly became the most dominantly advertised tire business on those mediums in his city. Not only did he become dominant as compared to other tire businesses, he eventually became one of the most dominant local advertisers on radio and television in his market. In a relatively short number of years, he became one of the largest if not the largest tire dealer in his market.

He became dominant in terms of number of locations, the cost of the locations, and the amount of advertising dollars he spent on his business. I watched this happen over a period of years and realized that what he did was really not that unusual. Businesses become dominant in their industry by being dominant in their marketing and advertising.

The question for our purposes is: Does the domination principle apply to Yellow Pages advertising as well? You know I am going to answer yes, but before I do so, let's return to our three hamburger giants for a comparison.

They have learned that good locations give them more exposure to potential customers. They have learned that the better the location, the more business they do. They measure a potential location in terms of traffic count and ease of access. They know what a good location is and what a bad location is in terms of their business. It is all a matter of traffic.

What is Yellow Pages usage? It is "eye traffic." Instead of cars driving down streets and highways, it is pairs of eyes looking for potential places to spend the money of their owners. The streets they are traveling are the pages they see when they are looking in the Yellow Pages. McDonald's isn't going to sell a hamburger to me if I don't stop into their restaurant. I am not going to stop into their restaurant if I don't see it because I am not on the street where it is located. A Yellow Pages user's eyes can't do business with you if they can't see you because they looking at another page rather than the page on which you are located.

So, is location important in Yellow Pages? Yes. Do some locations cost more than others? Yes. If you have a better location, do you have a better response? Yes.

Let's return to our fast-food chains again. In most cities of any size, such businesses usually have multiple locations—but they don't have to. In theory, they could build just one super location in the heart of a city and hopefully do as much business out of that one super location as they would do with multiple locations—but they don't do that. They dominate by having multiple locations as well as by having good locations to start with. With multiple locations, they are exposed to more traffic. The greater the traffic exposure, the higher their sales.

Are multiple locations important in Yellow Pages? The answer is yes. What are multiple locations in terms of Yellow Pages advertising? Today, in most markets of any size, there is more than one Yellow Pages publisher. Each publisher represents, if you will, an additional location. For most businesses and professionals, there is more than one heading to be considered for advertising in each directory. Printing companies can advertise under PRINTERS and COPYING SERVICE; fine restaurants can consider RESTAURANTS, CATERERS, and/or BANQUET ROOMS; and plumbers can appear under PLUMBING CONTRACTORS, PLUMBING DRAINS & SEWER CLEANING, as well as WATER HEATERS—REPAIRING. Each additional heading is like an additional location.

All of the Yellow Pages directory locations are not of equal value. Some directories have more traffic than others, and some headings have more traffic than others. Each location must be evaluated based on its potential to produce business. Whether you advertise or not and the degree to which you advertise determine the results you achieve from this traffic. The traveling eyes are going to buy from someone most of the time. The only question is who will get the business.

The most important way you dominate in Yellow Pages is by the size of the ad you buy. (By the way, the tire store mentioned earlier became even more dominant over the years in both the size and frequency of its ads as it added more and more locations. I have to believe the dollar return from the advertising increased as well.) You dominate in Yellow Pages by ad size in two ways. If there are no display ads under a heading you are considering, you either buy an in-column ad large enough to be the largest in-column ad under the heading or you buy a small display ad to give you the largest ad under the heading. When there are display ads under your heading, you buy as large an ad as necessary to have the largest ad under the heading. Sometimes you can achieve this with a one-eighth-page ad, sometimes a quarter page, sometimes a half, and sometimes you may have to buy a full-page ad to attain a degree of dominance.

The individual headings help to guide you in your decisions. They tell you how large an ad to buy to achieve your goal of dominance and at the same time tell you when the ad you are considering buying is too large. If there are existing three-quarter or full-page ads under your heading, you need to consider a full-page ad. If the largest ad is a quarter page, there is no need to consider a full page. That would be like a department store building a facility large enough to serve a population base of over one million in a market of 200,000 people. In both cases, that would be overkill.

If it is true that the size of the ad is important, why is it important? It all has to do with traffic—both the level of exposure to the traffic and the level of competition for exposure to the traffic.

The Yellow Pages Sampler which appears at the back of this book contains sample headings with a variety of ads. It will be referred to throughout the remainder of the book to illustrate certain points made in the text. Our first example illustrates the importance of size.

Let's start with a relatively simple example. If you turn to page Y-9 in The Yellow Pages Sampler, you will find the first page of the heading CATERERS. Pages Y-8 and Y-9 constitute what is called a spread-page. Like all spread-pages in a Yellow Pages directory, a certain amount of "eye traffic" lands on such a page in a day, a week, a month, or a year. The amount of that "eye traffic" is determined by the heading, the particular directory, and even the time of year. The time of year aspect is especially important to the CATERERS heading. The Christmas and New Year's holiday season causes a surge in the traffic under this heading.

Notice that the heading CATERERS only takes up one page of this spread-page. Also notice that there are three display ads on page Y-9. Let's assume that 100 calls are going to be placed to the companies with display ads on this page. The time period is of no importance in this illustration. It could be a day, several days, or a week. If the 100 calls were to be divided evenly among the three display ads, each would average approximately 33 calls.

Now turn to the next spread-page, pages Y-10 and Y-11. There is a total of nine display ads for caterers on this spread-page. (The tenth display ad is for a dome company and would have no effect on the calls received by caterers from this spread-page.) Once again, let's assume 100 calls will be placed to the companies with display ads on this spread-page. Each ad would average approximately 11 calls if the calls were divided equally.

At this point, you may be thinking that some of the "eye traffic" from the previous spread-page may have "turned the corner" and landed on this spread-page. You would be right. Some of it probably did. What we are concerned with is how the calls to the companies with ads on this spread-page are divided. From this example, it becomes clear that the more ads that appear on a spread-page, the fewer the average number of calls per ad. I call this "the traffic analysis."

The traffic analysis says results are affected by the number of competitors that have exposure to the same traffic as your ad. The more competitors, the more difficult it is for you to get a call. The fewer the competitors, the better your odds of getting a call.

Now turn to pages Y-2 and Y-3 under the heading CARPET & RUG DEALERS—NEW. Again, let's assume that 100 calls are going to be placed to the companies with display ads on this spread-page. That means an average of 25 calls per ad for the four half-page ads on this spread-page.

If you turn to pages Y-4 and Y-5, you will also find four display ads. Assuming that another 100 calls will be made to the companies with display ads on this spread-page, the average would also be 25 calls each. The number would actually be lower than for the previous spread-page because there are some additional in-column ads that potentially could pull some of the calls away from the display ads.

The last spread-page under this heading is on pages Y-6 and Y-7. There are six display ads on this spread-page. Using the same analysis as for the previous spread-pages, we can assume an average of approximately 16 calls or less per ad. Once again, there are in-column ads that would probably have the additional effect of lowering the number of calls per display ad.

Does this seem too simple? Consider this example from the perspective of a fast-food restaurant. Imagine a heavily traveled highway with a McDonald's restaurant and no other fast-food restaurant for miles. If 100 hamburgers are going to be sold on that block, McDonald's will sell all 100 of them.

Suppose a Burger King opens up directly across the street. Certainly it will draw some additional business to the block just by the fact it is there, but what do you suppose will happen to the 100 burgers that would have been bought only from McDonald's? Wouldn't some of them be bought from Burger King instead? Add a Wendy's just down the street, and some of the 100 burgers would be bought there as well. This just seems like simple logic.

Now suppose McDonald's could eliminate one of its competitors. Wouldn't the reverse of the above scenario happen? This would be another type of "the process of elimination." That is what happens when someone buys a larger ad. They eliminate some competition from their block, which in Yellow Pages terminology is called a spread-page. In fact, in the case of a full-page ad, obviously no competitive ads would appear on the same page. They could only appear on the following or preceding page.

If you turn to pages Y-14 and Y-15, you will find two full-page ads for PLUMBING CONTRACTORS. Assuming 100 calls will be placed to the companies with display ads on this spread-page, the average would be 50 calls per ad. Later in this book, you will learn that one of the full-page ads will probably get more calls than the other for some very good reasons. For now, try to guess which one that might be and why.

When you turn to pages Y-16 and Y-17, you will again find two display ads. One is a full-page ad and the other approximately a two-thirds-page ad. (By the way, the latter ad size is very rare. You will not find an ad of this size in most directories around the country, but it does exist in some.) Again, the average number of calls would be 50 per ad based on a total of 100 calls, but we would expect two things to affect the average. One is that the full-page ad precedes and is larger than the two-thirds-page ad. The other is the presence of additional in-column ads on this spread-page.

Pages Y-18 and Y-19 contain two two-thirds-page ads along with additional in-column ads. Therefore, the average number of calls per display ad would probably be less than the average for the preceding spread-page. Now turn to pages Y-20 and Y-21. This spread-page contains three display ads, which would average approximately 33 calls per ad. Turn the page again and you will find four display ads on pages Y-22 and Y-23, for an average of 25 calls each. Finally, you will find nine display ads sharing pages Y-24 and Y-25. Now the average number of calls is down to approximately 11 per ad.

And that is why larger ads attract more calls than smaller ads under the same heading. It is "the process of elimination." As mentioned previously, Yellow Pages users eliminate ads in the process of deciding whom to call. Advertisers also play a role in this process by not placing an ad on the page being viewed, thus eliminating themselves from "the process of elimination." Advertisers can play another role in this process through the size of the ad they buy. The larger the ad, the more competitors' ads that are eliminated from the choices that could potentially appear on a spread-page.

There are other ways to dominate in addition to having the largest ad under a given heading in one directory. If there is more than one directory serving your market, you can dominate with a dominant location in a second directory as well. Each directory represents its own separate "eye traffic," and the same principles apply. Frequently what it takes to be dominant under one heading in one directory differs from what it would take to dominate in another. That is why you should make your decisions one heading and one directory at a time.

Another way to dominate in Yellow Pages is to advertise under two or more headings in a given directory in a dominant way. A full-page ad for an air conditioning contractor under AIR CONDITIONING CONTRACTORS & SYSTEMS does a business no good whatsoever when someone is referring to HEATING CONTRACTORS. Therefore, in terms of exposure to additional traffic, an air conditioning contractor would be better off with an ad under both headings. The ads would probably not be the same size because the value of the headings would be different. The headings guide an advertiser by mirroring their relative importance.

So far, we have discussed dominating through ad size first and number of headings and number of directories second. There is another reason ad size is so important. Until you truly test the value of a heading, you will never know its value. Once you find that being dominant under a given heading is productive and worth the extra investment, you will be more likely to consider becoming dominant under more than one heading and/or in more than one directory. Throughout the remainder of this book, other suggestions will be offered to increase the return on investment for any ad you buy. It is important to emphasize at this point, however, that size is the main factor that determines results.

One of the most difficult aspects of the domination principle is the idea of using multiple ads under the same heading. Even though this aspect does not apply to most headings in Yellow Pages, it is important in terms of understanding what domination truly is.

In most directories, the largest ad available is a full-page ad. In some cases, it may be less than that (a half-page ad, for example). Once someone buys a full-page ad, there is a tendency for the buyer to believe that is the best he or she can do. That frequently is not the case. It is the best **single** thing the buyer can do under a heading. Headings that contain full-page ads consist of several pages of ads and listings. It is not unusual for such headings to consist of twenty pages or more in major metropolitan directories. This is where the concept of multiple ads comes into the picture.

The traffic analysis really applies when considering the use of multiple ads under a single heading. We have talked about the fact that some "eye traffic" turns pages. The result is that all of the calls to companies with ads under a heading are not placed to the companies with ads on the first page or two of a large heading. Remember, usage is "the process of elimination." One of the ways ads are eliminated is by the turning of pages, which means exposure to other ads. Because calls are placed to companies with ads on virtually every page within a heading, the only way an advertiser can get calls from a given page is to have an ad on that page. Some exceptional Yellow Pages advertisers truly understand this fact and take advantage of it by purchasing more than one ad under a heading.

To use this concept most successfully, the ads must be bought so that the advertiser has ads on more than one spread-page within a heading. Preferably the heading should be large enough so the ads fall several spread-pages apart. In most cases, this will mean that the second ad will be smaller than the first ad and will be placed further back in the heading. This means that the second ad, by being located on a different spread-page, has exposure which the first ad does not. The larger the heading, the easier it is to separate the ads so they do not compete with each other to any great extent.

As mentioned, very few advertisers even consider such a strategy, let alone put it into practice. If you really think about the concept of "eye traffic," you will realize that there is something to be gained by placing multiple ads under larger headings. Let's consider this in terms of our example of a fast-food chain. The larger the city, the more likely you are to find more than one McDonald's in it. That is because McDonald's realizes that one location cannot have exposure to all of the traffic within the city. Only by strategically locating additional restaurants can McDonald's take maximum advantage of the total population of the larger cities. The larger the city, the more locations it has.

This may not seem like an important strategy for many advertisers. However, if you are in a business or a profession in a metropolitan market where one or more of your headings contain many pages of relatively large ads, you need to look at the possibility of such a strategy. If you have one of the largest ads at the beginning of a heading, you should realize that smaller ads further back in the heading are getting calls as well. Some of these calls, perhaps many of them, are from users who did not see or passed by your larger ad. The smaller ads are not producing as many calls as your larger ad, but they are still producing calls. Every McDonald's does not have as good a location as all the others. Those with a better location do more business. The poorer locations certainly contribute to the profitability of McDonald's; they just don't make as great a contribution as the better locations do.

Even though larger ads are the most profitable, it is still important to recognize that smaller ads generate calls as well. Not every advertiser can be the dominant advertiser under a heading. There may even be good reasons why you should not have the largest ad. In that case, it is important to understand that smaller ads will produce fewer results, but they will produce some results. You cannot judge the results you might get from a larger ad by the results you are getting from a smaller ad. Each one produces what it will produce. It is up to you to decide what you want in terms of results.

If you still doubt the significance of size, try a couple of economical tests. The major reason most advertisers do not buy large Yellow Pages ads is the perception of cost. Bigger ads cost more than smaller ads; we all know that. The problem with that thinking is Yellow Pages ads are intended to produce revenue for their buyers. If an ad produces profitable results for its buyer, does it in fact cost or does it produce "the life blood of a business"? If an ad produces profitable results, should cost be less of a factor in the decision-making process? If you still doubt the value of size, you are still thinking in the cost mode rather than the revenue mode.

One way to change your thinking is to find a relatively inexpensive place to buy an ad that would be dominant under its heading. One way to accomplish this is to advertise in a smaller directory that serves a segment of your market. Because directory rates are essentially based upon the number of copies distributed, an ad in a directory with a smaller distribution will cost less than an ad in a directory with a much larger distribution. Smaller directories also tend to be less competitive in terms of the number of competitors that appear under a given heading. What this may mean is that you do not have to buy as large an ad to be dominant under a heading in a smaller directory. The combination of a smaller ad coupled with a lower cost per inch for ad space means a much lower price to test the domination principle. When you see how it works in the smaller, less expensive directory, it should be easier for you to consider spending a much greater amount to be dominant in a much larger directory.

If a suitable smaller directory is not available or if you choose not to consider a smaller directory for some reason, you can test the importance of size another way. Not all headings are equal in their income-producing capability for their advertisers. The less productive headings attract fewer and smaller ads than those that are more productive for their advertisers. Choose a secondary heading relevant to your business or practice and use it to prove the value of size before you risk buying a larger ad under a more competitive heading. Printers can do this under COPYING SERVICE. Automobile repair shops can do this under BRAKE SERVICE, ROAD SERVICE, or any number of smaller headings. Attorneys can do this under the specialty headings that exist in many directories today.

If you still doubt the value of size, you have missed the most important message in this book. Ask yourself why certain headings contain a lot of large ads. Ask yourself why movers, florists, personal injury attorneys, plumbing contractors, and automobile insurance agents spend the amount of money they do not just in your local directory, but in virtually any directory of any size around the country. Are the consistent buyers of larger ads under such competitive headings wrong, or do they know something about size the majority of their competitors don't know? You can learn a great deal more about the value of Yellow Pages advertising from your competitors who buy big ads than you ever will from those who buy small ads or no ads at all.

If you still doubt the importance of size, the next chapter should encourage you to reconsider your opinion.

5

A TALE OF FOUR BUSINESSES

This chapter is about four people in the same type of business operating in the same general market. It illustrates the differences in the opinions of the fours owners, the differences in the make-up of their businesses, the differences in the size and profitability of their businesses, and, most importantly, the differences in the way they view the Yellow Pages.

All four eventually became full-page advertisers. The largest of the four competed directly with the other three. Two of the three smaller businesses were located in suburbs north of the major city in the market, and the third was located in the south section of the market.

The owner of business number one started his business about six years ago. Like many small business owners, he started his business out of his home. He bought a three-quarter-page ad his first year, after some considerable encouragement from me. Prior to the close of the directory, he called and asked me to come back to see him. He said he needed to make some changes in his ad. When I came to see him, he told me he had second thoughts about the ad. He thought it was way too big for a one-truck service business and was afraid he would never be able to pay for the ad. I eventually convinced him he would pay for the ad with the money he would make from it.

When I called him the following year, I asked him how things were going. His first words to me were, "God bless you, Tom." I will never forget those words. Obviously, the ad was doing what it was supposed to be doing. As a result of its effectiveness, he increased the ad to a full page for the following year.

Two years later, he added color to the ad. My sales manager was with me when I called on him and observed to the customer that I really had not worked very hard for the sale since it was the customer's idea to add red to the ad. The customer replied, "Tom worked very hard for that sale several years ago." I tell you this not to brag but to set the stage for what was to come.

As his business grew, the owner became increasingly involved in doing new construction work. While Yellow Pages advertising is very effective in producing service business for this type of contractor, he believed he needed to produce additional business by doing new construction work. New construction work can produce a large amount of income compared to the service part of this type of business. The negative side is that the profit margins are small as a result of competitive bidding to get the work. In addition, the cash flow is usually slow and the accounts receivable are high.

The business continued to grow. The owner added trucks, men, and a commercial manager to help him run his new construction department. Eventually, the latter employee got him to the point of near bankruptcy. The business he brought in, while large in dollars, proved to be unprofitable and difficult to collect. The owner was forced to downsize his company and essentially get out of the new construction business. He had such a poor cash flow situation that it was difficult for him to pay his telephone bill, which included the cost of his Yellow Pages advertising.

When it came time to renew his ad, he told me he had to reduce it drastically. He was under pressure from all sides: his wife, his accountant, and the telephone company. It was hard for me not to give in to feelings of sympathy in a situation like this, but I knew that he would lose much more in income than he would save in expense if he reduced his ad substantially.

Two things kept him from making the drastic move. He had a great deal of faith in me, and the business was small enough that he knew almost every call he was getting from his ad and the income he was deriving from it. I urged him to look at the income versus the cost of the ad. Would he be better off without the expense of the ad if he lost the income it produced? I pointed out to him that his problem was not the cost of the ad. It was the deep hole he had dug for himself in other ways that was creating the financial stress. The net income from the ad was actually slowly helping him get out of the hole. He kept his full-page ad.

About two years after business number one's owner bought his first three-quarter-page ad, the owner of business number two bought the assets of another company that served the same market as business number one. Among the assets he wanted were the telephone numbers owned by the company he purchased. To get these numbers, he had to assume the cost of any ads billed to them. One of the ads was a three-quarter-page ad in the directory where business number one now had a full-page ad.

The owner of business number two was not a believer in Yellow Pages advertising. It had not played even the smallest part in the building of his business to this point. He had only been in business for five years, and he was already one of the largest businesses of his type in his metropolitan market. He had built the business by aggressively pursuing new construction work. Therefore, when he assumed the telephone numbers of the company he had bought, he was, in effect, buying advertising he did not believe had any value.

He was pleasantly surprised when he discovered the advertising was indeed profitable. As a result of his experience with a smaller suburban directory, he started buying full-page ads in the two larger directories that served the major part of his market. As of this writing, he has full-page ads in three directories in his market.

About the time business number two started to get results from its newly acquired Yellow Pages advertising, business number three was started in the home of its owner in the same area as business number one. In this case, I was not able to convince the owner to start out aggressively. (By now, I'm sure you know I tried!) He bought an eighth-page ad because, like most businesses, he was more concerned with the price of the ad than the true potential income that was there for the taking.

When I returned the following year, owner number three was not raving about his results, nor did he have any strong, positive feelings about me. I asked him about the calls he did receive. He knew he had profited from the ad, but not to any degree that had made a major impact on his business. Since he did profit from the ad, I was able to persuade him to spend more to get more. Being quite conservative, he decided to buy a quarter-page ad.

My visit the next year was the same as the previous year. Yes, he had gotten more calls than the previous year. Yes, the quarter-page ad was more profitable than the eighth-page ad. No, it still did not affect his business as greatly as he needed it to be affected.

This time I convinced him that he was doing things the hard way. If he had felt confident the first year that he would have profited more from a quarter-page ad than an eighth-page ad, he would have started out with the quarter-page ad. Hindsight is always clearer than foresight. So he went against his conservative nature and decided to buy a three-quarter-page ad. (By this time, business number one and business number two had full-page ads.) He realized that his conservative approach resulted in painfully slow growth for his business and that it was now time to really go after more of what he needed.

As a result of a significant increase in results from the three-quarter-page ad, he bought a full-page ad for the following issue and has had the full-page ad for three years as of this writing. His business still is not as large as business number two, but it is growing at a much faster rate now.

A couple of years after the start-up of business number three, business number four was started in the largest city in the market. Once again, the owner started the business in his home. The problem was that the directories serving his city were much more expensive than the directory serving the northern suburbs of his market. As we talked, he decided that the most he could spend was $400 per month. Since a full-page ad at a discounted rate would have cost about $1,800 per month, he was not going to get a very large ad for his money. In addition, his heading was extremely competitive in this directory, with five or six full-page ads and several three-quarter-page ads.

I asked him if he would be willing to concentrate his business in the south suburbs of his market. He said he would go anyplace as long as he made money. I told him I did not want him to spend $400 per month in the larger directory. When he asked why, I told him that $400 per month would get him a three-quarter-page ad in the smaller directory serving the south suburbs. I told him he would get a much better return dollar for dollar with a larger ad in the smaller directory than he would with a smaller ad in the larger directory.

He believed me and liked the idea of being aggressive with the limited amount he was willing to spend. His goal was to build his business as fast as he could, and if that meant focusing on the south suburbs, he was willing to do so.

Well, I am sure you can guess what happened. The ad worked. He greeted me enthusiastically and appreciatively the next year. He was very receptive to my recommendation that he buy a full-page ad in the directory for the following year.

Just after he bought the full-page ad, he moved his business out of his home and rented commercial space in the south section of his market. Part of his plan was to prepare for future growth to the north of this location. To accomplish that, he decided to buy an aggressive ad in the larger directory he had considered to be too expensive his first year. It always held the potential to make him more money than the smaller directory. It was his experience with the aggressive approach in the smaller directory that convinced him to do what he needed to do to achieve that potential.

There are some obvious lessons to be learned from this tale. Aggressiveness does pay in the Yellow Pages if you are in the right business, as these four businesses were. Being conservative, especially during the start-up period of a business, only holds you back. Starting a business is a painful process, especially for the owner who needs to take personal income from the business. The faster a business builds it revenues, the sooner an owner can earn his or her living from it.

There is an untold side to this tale. These four businesses have dozens of competitors who think they are wrong in buying such large ads. They voice their opinions every year by not buying large ads to compete with these four. Many of these competitors would compete if they were convinced it would be best for their businesses. Why don't they? Some of them haven't had the right Yellow Pages salesperson to convince them that they should. Some have made up their mind—and that is it! Most are hung up on the cost of large ads.

If you are in a business or profession that has large ads under your heading(s), I hope you now realize the potential the heading has. If you already are aggressive, I congratulate you on being in the minority. If you are not aggressive and should be, I hope this tale helps convince you to change your approach to Yellow Pages advertising. If it does, then you have taken an important step toward building your business.

6
BUYING STRATEGIES

Frequently, buying Yellow Pages advertising is not as simple as buying a single ad in a single directory. For most businesses and professions, there is more than one heading to be considered. Often, there is more than one directory to be considered as well. Add to this the fact that many directory publishers have some rather complicated marketing plans and discount programs, and you are faced with a potentially complicated decision-making process. Effective buying of Yellow Pages advertising requires a buying strategy with the objective of producing profitable results from the ads.

The first strategy is to eliminate some directories from consideration. If a directory covers a geographical market you do not want to cultivate, eliminate it. In this day and age of multiple directories covering the same market, you may decide to eliminate one or more of the directories that serve your market. In most cases, the one directory you would not eliminate is the directory published by the local telephone company that serves your market. I know of no major market in the country where the local telephone company directory is used less than one of its competitor's directories. The Yellow Pages industry has changed and continues to change rapidly, but as of the writing of this book, the most frequently used directories in this country are those published by the local telephone companies.

If I had written this book ten years ago, I would have given very little space to the subject of competitive directories. But this recent change in the industry has made the decision-making process much more complicated. Two major changes have occurred in the publishing of Yellow Pages directories. Non-telephone-company publishers have appeared on the scene in ever-increasing numbers, and telephone companies have started distributing directories outside of their area of telephone service responsibility. The result of these changes is the growth of directories being published to serve the same markets in community after community throughout the United States.

Historically, directories were published by local telephone companies and were provided by those companies to their customers. For example, the Harrisburg, Pennsylvania directory was published by Bell of Pennsylvania for customers of its Harrisburg telephone business office, just as the Orlando, Florida directory was distributed to customers of Southern Bell's Orlando business office. Prior to the spin-off of the Bell telephone companies from AT&T, relatively few areas of the country were served by more than one directory publisher. Some independent publishers tried to compete with the local telephone companies, but for the most part they were of little consequence.

Since the breakup of AT&T, however, the number of competitors has grown quite rapidly. As you might suspect, some have been more successful than others, and they merit greater consideration as a potential source of business. The problem comes in determining how successful these publishers are in competing against the local telephone company. Success is measured by usage. The greater the percentage of usage achieved in a market by a given directory, the more successful that publisher will be in delivering customers for its advertisers.

The problem is that there is no reliable source available in most markets to tell you the relative usage of the various directories serving those markets. So how do you decide whether or not to advertise in one of these competing directories? The first rule of thumb is if a directory is being published for the first time, don't advertise in it. Just because someone decides to publish a directory does not mean the directory will be successful in delivering a satisfactory amount of business for its advertisers. Therefore, the best strategy is to make the publisher prove its ability to produce results over time. If it is successful, you will see that success mirrored over a period of years. If it is successful, it will retain a substantial amount of the advertising it sold in the previous issue and you will see the growth of its advertiser base. When you do not see this happen, you will be glad you did not support it with your advertising dollars.

But there will be situations where you will want to advertise in competing directories. Which ones and to what degree are the natural questions at this point. First, if a directory has been published in an area for five or more years, it is a fairly safe bet that it is producing results for at least some of its advertisers. It does so by taking usage from its competitors. A user may have more than one directory available, but it is the directory being used at a specific time that is delivering that user to its advertisers.

To what degree you want to go after the usage of a particular directory is determined by how much usage you know or think it is getting. I wish I could tell you to rely on the publisher to tell you. Unfortunately, you will be given accurate usage information only some of the time. There is no magic way to determine the accuracy of the information you are given. When I buy Yellow Pages advertising for my clients, nothing makes me angrier than to see conflicting usage claims being made by competing publishers. There is some truth in the usage information of each directory, but what is it?

You and I, therefore, have to rely upon what our eyes tell us and on some common sense. There are few areas in the country where the publishers will be equally good at getting usage for their advertisers. Usually, the local telephone company will be the leader in terms of usage. Therefore, what we need to determine is how much usage the competing directory is getting. This can be done by observing what happens to the larger ads in the directory as subsequent issues are published. Remember, it is the larger ads in the directory that are getting the greatest results. The owners of those ads try to monitor them closely because they are spending a relatively large amount of money to achieve those results. When larger ads are retained and new ads are added over a period of years, that is an indication the directory is getting sufficient usage to support such ads.

Let's assume the local telephone company is getting 70% of the usage in a market and its competitor is getting the remaining 30% of the usage. If the rates for the competing directory are less than half the cost of the telephone company's directory, you have a potentially good buy available to you in the competing directory. Usually, the amount of advertising done by your competitors will be substantially less in the competing directory. This means you will have an easier time being dominant under your heading and the cost of being dominant will be less. A half-page ad in the competing directory will not have to deliver as much business as a half-page ad in the more expensive directory. If it does, it will be a very good buy for you.

Your decision should focus on the extent to which you want to attempt to get a substantial amount of business from this directory. This is really the main factor in your decision about any directory you are considering. You should consider advertising in what appears to be the less frequently used directory when:

1 You are a new business and the next directory to be delivered in your market is the less frequently used directory. There are two advantages to be considered. First, this directory can deliver business to you sooner than its competitor with the greater usage. How much sooner is an important consideration as well. Second, you will start out spending less to go after the business you need.

2 You want to go after business through the Yellow Pages in an aggressive way, but you do not want to commit to what it would cost to be dominant in the larger directory. It is easier to take advantage of your competitors' ignorance in these directories. Frequently, more of them ignore these directories. Remember, there is a direct correlation between total usage of a directory and what it can potentially bring you. Like any other advertising medium, if its rates are cheaper, there is a reason for it. It takes big results for a medium to justify larger rates over time.

3 You have substantial advertising in the major directory and are looking for an additional source of business. In the previous example, 30% is not as attractive as 70%, but it can still be a substantial amount of usage. In this case, if you are aggressive in the major directory, it will be easy for you to decide to be aggressive in the smaller directory as well, provided the pricing is relative to the usage.

4 You are concerned that you are losing business because of lack of representation in the less frequently used directory. The more established your company, the more this should concern you. This is what I call the defensive approach to Yellow Pages advertising. A major Yellow Pages advertiser who owned a very successful company once said to me: "I'm not concerned about what I get out of Yellow Pages as much as I am concerned about what I wouldn't get if I wasn't there." If you are not there, you give your competitors the opportunity to literally steal business from you. You probably do not allow that to happen in other ways that you get business if you can help it. The more important Yellow Pages advertising is to your business, the less you would want that to happen in Yellow Pages.

If none of these scenarios fits your particular situation, you may just decide to take the free listing most of these publishers offer. If your Yellow Pages representative does not offer you a free listing, question him or her about it. It is usually available. If a free listing is not available, you must then decide if the directory is worthy of some sort of minimal representation by your company.

The decision-making process is the same no matter what directory you are considering. Once you have decided to advertise in a directory, there are certain points you need to address. The first is what headings you want to consider for some sort of representation. Ask yourself what specific customers you are trying to attract. There is no sense advertising under a heading that would deliver customers you do not want. One of the major advantages of Yellow Pages advertising is the opportunity to change your business. It can do this by bringing you additional customers and therefore helping you grow. More than that, it can bring you more of a specific type of customer that you may want. For example, a copy machine dealer can increase fax machine sales by advertising under the heading FACSIMILE EQUIPMENT. If the dealer is not interested in building this part of the business to any great extent, then he or she may decide to advertiser under this heading in a minimal or near minimal way.

Let your eyes tell you the potential for the Yellow Pages to deliver specific customers to you. Ten years ago, the Yellow Pages could not deliver much fax machine business for anybody, and the directories showed it. There was very little advertising under the headings relating to fax machines. But the market for fax machines has grown tremendously since then and so has the ability of Yellow Pages to deliver some of that market to its advertisers. The result has been a growth in those headings in recent years.

What you are trying to determine is the degree to which you should advertise under a given heading. This is determined by two considerations. The first is your purpose in advertising there in the first place. If you are advertising under a heading because you think you must be there but you do not want to attract too many customers, then some type of a listing or small in-column ad is probably appropriate. If you are trying to get as much business as possible from a heading, then a more aggressive approach should be used.

What you see should help you determine what size ad to buy. The easiest way to determine how big of an ad to buy is to buy as large of an ad as it will take to be the largest ad under a particular heading. For maximum results, that is the best decision. But there are a lot of reasons why you might not decide to buy the largest ad under the heading. The most common reason is the cost of the ad. There are times when that is a good reason and there are times when it is not. In any event, everyone is not going to buy the largest ad under their heading, and everyone should not always buy the largest ad.

Chapter 6 • Buying Strategies

There is no one ad that is the right ad to buy under any given heading. If you do not have the largest ad under a heading, it does not mean you are going to go out of business. On the other hand, if you have the largest ad under a heading, that does not mean you won't go out of business. You should expect to profit from whatever representation you have. You almost always get calls from even the smallest ads and listings. The difference will be in the quantity and the quality of the calls. A steak house with an eighth-of-a-page ad located on the tenth page of the RESTAURANTS heading will get business from the ad, but it won't get as much business as it would have gotten with a half-page ad on the second page of the heading.

Let's look at a heading in The Yellow Pages Sampler to consider some possible decisions. For now, we will ignore the use of color in the ads and look at our choices in terms of the size of the ad we would be purchasing for our money. On page Y-13, you will find the heading PHYSICIANS & SURGEONS—M.D.—SURGERY—HAND. The largest ads under this very small heading are two one-inch ads. This means that the doctor who purchased a one-and-a-half-inch or a two-inch ad would have the dominant ad under the heading. The heading does not call for a display ad because of the size of the ads and the number of ads that currently appear under it. The doctor should not expect to add a patient a week from such an ad. A patient or two a year will probably more than pay for the ad. Anything more than that would increase its profitability.

This was a very simple example. On page Y-8, you will find the heading CASH REGISTERS & SUPPLIES. There are four display ads as well as some in-column ads and listings under this heading. If the decision is to dominate the heading, the ad we would consider would be a quarter-page ad. It would have been the first and largest ad under this heading and would have moved the ad for Cash Register Medic down. Assuming we decide not to buy the largest ad, there are still some interesting choices.

If we had purchased a 3/16-page ad, like Cash Register Medic, our ad would have appeared immediately below its ad and would have moved down the ad for Premier Hospitality Service. This would have cost us about one-third less than the quarter-page ad and we would have had the second ad under the heading.

If we had purchased an eighth-page ad, like Premier has, we would have appeared immediately below Premier's ad and would have moved down the ad for ABD Equipment. We would have had the third ad under the heading and our cost would have been half of the cost of the quarter-page ad.

The next two ads are 3/32-page ads. If we had purchased one of them, our ad would have appeared in the lower right-hand corner of the page, where you see the two spaces marked filler. We would have had the last display ad under the heading. There is another choice, however, which does not appear on this page. There is a display ad smaller than a 3/32. It is a 1/16 page. It would appeared in the same area where our 3/32-page ad would have appeared. It would have been 50% smaller, but the position would have been the same and the cost would have been 50% less.

In this case, if money is the deciding factor, a 1/16-page ad would not be a bad buy for the first time under this heading. It would have as good a position as the 3/32-page ad and would be located very close to where the 1/8-page ad would have appeared. Because it is located on the same page as and is contiguous to the larger display ads under the heading, it profits from the attention-getting capabilities of the larger ads and should get reasonably good readership.

I call this "the best buy analysis." My first choice is always to buy the largest ad under a heading. When that is not an option, I then look for an ad size that gets comparatively good position for the money. Under this heading, we could have done a similar analysis in terms of an in-column ad if the decision was not to go with a display ad for some reason.

Now let's look at the heading PRINTERS on pages Y-26 through Y-28. As you can see, the decisions get more complicated as the size and number of ads increase. It would have taken a half-page ad to be the first ad under this heading. It would have appeared where Formula Printing Services' ad appears and Melvin Printing's ad would have moved to page Y-27.

If we had bought a 3/8-page ad, like Formula Printing and Melvin Printing, our ad would have appeared in the top left-hand corner of page

Y-27, where Speedy Printing Service has a quarter-page ad. If we had purchased a quarter-page ad, it would have appeared in the upper right-hand corner of page Y-28. If we had purchased a 3/16-page ad, it could have appeared in the lower left- or right-hand corner, where Printer's Alley and Kwik Printing have 1/8-page ads. If we had purchased a 1/8-page ad, it would have appeared on the following page.

I like the 3/8-page and the 1/4-page ads as choices in this example. I like them for reasons of positioning and space for copy. I would not discourage the purchase of either size, but I would still opt for the half-page ad if optimum results is the goal.

Sometimes, even in larger headings, some of the smaller ads stand out as good choices. That is because of the number of ads of various sizes to be considered. To illustrate this, let's look at the PLUMBING CONTRACTORS heading starting on page Y-14. There are three full-page ads. If we had purchased a full-page ad at the close of this directory last year, we would have had the fourth full-page ad, and it would have appeared on page Y-17.

Farragut Plumbing's ad is an unusual size. It is approximately two-thirds of a page. A three-quarter-page ad size is also available in this directory. This means that if we had purchased a three-quarter-page ad last year, it would have appeared on page Y-17. We would have attained the same position with the three-quarter-page ad that we would have attained with the purchase of a full-page ad. On a short-term basis, that is a very good buy.

If we had purchased a two-thirds-page ad, it would have appeared after the existing two-thirds-page ads. This means that our ad would have appeared on page Y-21. That's quite a move back for the difference between a three-quarter-page ad and a two-thirds-page ad. It makes the three-quarter-page ad look like a good buy when compared with the two-thirds-page ad.

If we had purchased a half-page ad, it would have appeared in the bottom left-hand corner of page Y-23, where Daniel's Plumbing has a 3/8-page ad. If we had purchased a 3/8-page ad, it would have appeared on page

Y-24 in the lower left-hand corner. The purchase of a quarter-page ad would have placed us in the upper right-hand corner of page Y-25. The quarter-page ad would have been a comparatively good buy. As you can see, smaller ads, such as 3/16-page and 1/8-page ads, would fall even farther back in the heading.

This type of analysis does work. I use it when I buy for my clients, and I attain the position I am seeking the majority of the time. Every time I do, I achieve the position at a savings for my client. I recently used this approach for a client who placed three-quarter-page ads in three separate directories. In all three cases, his ads ended up on the same pages they would have appeared on had he bought full-page ads. However, as I mentioned, this is a short-term strategy. It must be re-evaluated each year. As for my client with the three three-quarter-page ads, he now must consider moving to full-page ads to secure his future position. If he stays with the three-quarter-page ads, additional full-page ads will keep pushing him further and further back in his heading. Since he is located in a growth market, there is a good chance of that happening to him over the next several years if he stands pat with the three-quarter-page ads.

The preceding examples apply to directories that use a seniority basis to determine ad position. All directories place the largest ads first. In the seniority system, two or more ads of the same size are placed in order of seniority. Seniority is not determined based on how long a company has been in business. It is based on when companies originally bought a particular size ad. If one company bought its ad four years ago and has renewed it ever since and another company buys its ad for the first time this year, the four-year buyer will be placed ahead of the other buyer.

Another method used to determine ad placement is alphabetical order. While this method is always used to determine the placement of in-column ads and listings, it is used more rarely in the determination of the placement of display ads. In this system, if your name precedes a competitor's name alphabetically, your display ad will precede your competitor's if both ads are the same size. Whether or not you think this method of placement is fair, it is important that you understand it and use it to your advantage rather than have it work against you.

If the name of your company is Allan Parks Repair Service, it will usually be listed in the White Pages as Parks Allan Repair Service. If you buy a display ad under this name, the ad will be placed with ads of the same size as if your name began with the letter P. There are two strategies you can use to work to your advantage rather than your disadvantage in this situation. You can tell the telephone company to list your firm name in the A section of the White Pages as Allan Parks Repair Service. Or you can establish what is known as an additional listing so you will be listed in both the A section and the P section of the White Pages. In either case, make sure you buy your display ad for the A-listed name so it helps your placement in a directory that uses alphabetical placement.

The best buy analysis can also be used in directories that use the alphabetical placement method for display ads. The closer your name is to the beginning of the heading, the better placement you will be able to attain for any size display ad. If you do have such a name, you will actually be able to jump ahead of existing ads of the same size that follow you in alphabetical order.

It is important to view each directory and each heading you are considering as an opportunity to get customers. You want the Yellow Pages to be profitable for you. The more money you want to make, the better you must be at utilizing these opportunities. Even if you are currently a Yellow Pages advertiser, it is probably safe to assume that you are nowhere near achieving your total business potential from the Yellow Pages. The limitations are limitations you have placed upon the product, not limitations in the product's ability to deliver customers or clients to you.

The limitations you should place on utilizing the Yellow Pages should be limitations related to the number of customers you want, the kinds of customers you want, and the geographical area(s) you want to serve. The Yellow Pages is a tool for achieving your goals. Its ability to deliver for certain types of businesses has been proven time and time again. It mirrors its ability to deliver for your type of business. You see that ability reflected in the number and size of ads under a heading in a given directory. Find out what the directory is telling you, and use these buying strategies to help you achieve your goals.

As mentioned earlier, there are times when you can put your money to better use by not buying color in a large display ad. In major markets, the addition of color to half-page or larger ads will add hundreds of dollars per month to the cost of the ad. This does not necessarily mean that the cost is not justified, but the odds are you will not be spending as much as you could or even should be spending. Since that is probably the case, it is a matter of putting the money you are willing to spend to its best use. It is not always wise to put all your eggs in one basket. Spending your entire budget under one heading or in one directory can leave additional sources of business unutilized. If you are considering adding color to a large display ad, it might be better to take those dollars and spend them under an additional heading(s) or in an additional directory. A full-page color ad under a heading may be your best choice under that particular heading, but it won't bring you one dollar's worth of business from the customer who is looking under another heading or in another directory.

As noted earlier, there are times when you may want to consider multiple ads under the same heading. The money you would spend for color in a full-page ad can help you to use such a strategy. All that gets in the way of such a buying strategy is usually the advertiser's willingness to spend the extra money. An incident involving the opposite situation will help to illustrate this point.

An advertiser in one of the largest cities in the United States had a dozen or more ads under a single heading. In fact, he had multiple ads under several headings in many directories in his metropolitan market. Without getting into how he bought so many ads under the same heading, the telephone company decided that he was monopolizing some of the headings, which was against its advertising policy. He was told he would have to cut his advertising in half in order for it to be acceptable to the publisher. He took the publisher to court, in effect demanding to spend more money than the publisher wanted him to spend. The publisher was saying, "We don't want your money!" The advertiser lost the case. The majority of his competitors thought he was crazy to spend that much money in the first place. Only he knew how much the judge cost him when he was ordered to reduce his Yellow Pages expenditures.

Again, it is important to note that businesses limit the product much more than they should. Every worthwhile product serves a purpose for its customers, in addition to providing revenue for the owner of the business. Products that do not serve that purpose either fail or are considered to be scams. Yellow Pages directories make a lot of money for their publishers—billions of dollars, in fact. They provide worthwhile information for the users of the directories as well. But the real money to be made is made by the advertisers who get business from the users of those directories. Directories that fail to deliver profitable business to their advertisers eventually fail. Most Yellow Pages do not fail. In fact, most have been around for decades. That means they are producing profitable results for their advertisers as a whole. If you limit what you spend on Yellow Pages because you think it won't affect your income, you are only fooling yourself.

Because of the increased competitive situation in most major markets today, most Yellow Pages publishers offer buying incentive or marketing plans to their advertisers. These plans are designed, for the most part, to give you a discount for what you buy today, with an increase in the cost (or a reduction in the discount, whichever way you want to look at it) the following year. If you are like most Yellow Pages advertisers, you probably dislike these plans. Perhaps if you knew the history of such plans, you would change your view of them.

Before competition began, the Yellow Pages industry was essentially a conglomeration of small monopolies. Each directory was the only directory in a market. As such, publishers felt free to raise their rates year after year. During the 1970s in particular, many publishers thought nothing of raising their rates 10% or more year after year. Since an advertiser had no other Yellow Pages directory to turn to, there was little choice but to accept the rates if the advertiser was going to continue to benefit from the Yellow Pages.

As competition started in various markets, the established publishers had to think twice before raising their rates. To start with, rates in competing directories were usually lower. Established publishers certainly did not want to give their advertisers additional reason for abandoning their product. In addition to being cheaper, the new competitors frequently offered discount buying plans to encourage advertisers to try their products. When these plans had some success in attracting advertisers, all publishers started to examine whether or not they should offer similar plans.

In terms of the established Yellow Pages directories published by the local telephone companies, two things happened. First, they lowered their average rate increases, if they decided to raise the rates at all for a particular issue. If they do increase their rates today, the increases are generally in the range of 3 to 5% per year. That has kept the rates down over the years and certainly has benefited the advertisers in such directories. Second, the addition of various discount plans in effect rolled back the rates to some extent. Gone are the days when everyone paid full price for every Yellow Pages ad they bought. Today, it is not unusual to buy Yellow Pages advertising for sixty cents on the dollar. This is especially true if the buyer understands the plans and uses them to his or her advantage. A buyer who pays somewhere between sixty and seventy cents on the dollar has gotten a good buy.

The plans differ by publisher and to some degree may change from year to year. It would be impossible to cover every type of discount plan, but some of the more frequently used plans are discussed in the following sections.

STEP-UP

Step-up is designed to encourage advertisers to increase the size of their ads. Some publishers offer this program only for display ads, while others offer it for in-column space ads as well as display ads. Step-up usually applies to any size ad as long as it is a new ad being bought by a new business or a buyer that has not advertised before. For existing advertisers, it is a little more complicated.

An advertiser with an existing display ad under a heading is usually required to buy an ad two sizes larger than the existing ad to qualify for step-up. Let's say an advertiser has a 1/16-page ad (usually called a quarter-column ad). Let's also assume the next two sizes are a 3/32 and a 1/8-page ad. If the advertiser buys a 1/8-page ad, the advertiser will pay the cost of a 3/32-page ad for one year. That means the advertiser would be paying approximately 75% of the full rate for the 1/8-page ad. Should the advertiser decide to buy an even larger ad than 1/8 page, step-up would still apply. In other words, if the advertiser bought a quarter-page ad instead of just a 1/8 page, the quarter-page ad would be billed at the rate of a 3/16-page ad for one year.

Frequently, step-up is a two-year program. That means the advertiser can renew the ad the second year without paying full rate for the ad. The discount is reduced the second year to about half of what it was the first year. Should the advertiser buy the ad for a third year in a row, then the full rate would be charged. In the third year, the advertiser usually has several options. First, the ad can be renewed for full price. Second, if the advertiser does not want to pay full price, the ad can be reduced to a size with a price more acceptable to the advertiser. Third, in some directories with step-up, the advertiser can move to the next size ad for the same price as it would cost to renew the existing ad. In the third situation, the advertiser is getting more space for the money but is also subject to additional increases in the cost of the new size ad over the following two years.

This program bothers far more advertisers than it should. The best advice is to make the best buy you can one year at a time. Don't even think about what will happen to the discount the following year. When the next year rolls around, look at your options at that time and again make the best buy you can. The discounts that are offered are real. There is always someone paying full price for the ad you are buying at a discount. Therefore, the more ads you buy at a discount, the better buy you are making.

EARLY CLOSE INCENTIVES

Some publishers offer incentives if you buy, renew, or increase your advertising by a certain date during their sales campaign. These publishers have found that such plans help them to get a higher percentage of their advertisers to contract for the next issue at an early date, which has always been a problem for publishers of large directories. Many people tend to put off their decision as long as possible. When too many advertisers do so, the result is a log jamb of work for the publisher in the closing weeks of a directory.

Normally these incentives do not apply if your are reducing your advertising. As a result, they are not only an incentive to handle your advertising earlier but can also be an incentive to keep or increase what you have. In any case, some publishers offer rather substantial incentives in the form of free ads or additional discounts. You should always take advantage of these plans if they are available. They make your buy a better one. In addition, it is to your advantage to buy early. You can expect greater service in terms of offering suggested layouts and proofs of the ads you order. The sales representatives have more time for each customer they see at the beginning of a campaign since most advertisers are not willing to negotiate early. In the closing stages of sales campaigns, the sales representatives are loaded down with callbacks as well as seeing all of the advertisers who have put them off until the closing weeks of the campaign. Studies conducted by publishers indicate that the rate of printing errors goes up significantly in the latter stages of a campaign because of the heavy workload. In addition, when buying a display ad for the first time, your positioning can potentially be improved when you buy early.

BUY ONE, GET ONE

This is an interesting plan. As an example, one advertiser was told that if he paid full rate for one display ad, the publisher would give him the same size ad (up to a half page) for free. In other words, if he bought a half-page ad at the full rate, he would get a free half page under another heading. If he bought a full-page ad at the full rate, he would also get a free half page. In this case, the advertiser had an existing half-page ad which was in its first year of step-up and he had a quarter-page ad under another heading. It would have actually cost him less to pay the full rate for the half-page ad and get another half page for free than it would have cost him to renew his half-page and quarter-page ads. As a result, he replaced his quarter-page ad with the free half-page ad and bought both of them for fifty cents on the dollar. The publisher will charge him 25% for the second half page next year, 50% the following year, 75% the year after that, and the full rate if he keeps the ad for the fifth year. A lot of things can happen between now and then. He decided to review his plan one year at a time. For now, I think you will agree he got an excellent buy.

ADDITIONAL DIRECTORY DISCOUNTS

Many publishers now offer discounts on any ad you buy in a second directory. These offers vary by publisher, but the discounts are real. Most advertisers in Yellow Pages could actually advertise in directories they do not utilize now. These plans are intended to give them an additional incentive to reconsider their previous buying decisions. Once again, these are true discounts. In some cases, you can buy into another directory at a lower rate than advertisers who have been advertising in it for years because it is their main directory.

There are times when this plan can truly be an extraordinary buy. One advertiser recently considered three directories published by a publisher that offered this plan. The advertiser was located in a town covered by the smallest of the three directories. The plan required him to pay the full rate for ads he placed in this directory. He would then receive a 35% discount on any ads he bought in the two larger, more expensive directories. He couldn't pass that offer up, especially since the markets covered by the two larger directories were very important to him.

FREE COUPONS

Most advertisers never buy a coupon in a telephone directory. Sometimes that is because their publisher does not have a coupon section. Nevertheless, coupons are fairly common in Yellow Pages directories today. Publishers frequently use them as an incentive to buy certain ads or to spend a certain amount of money with them. Coupons offer several advantages. First, of course, they are tangible. You can count them. Second, they can be used to compare the usage of two or more directories when you have equal advertising programs and coupon offers in them. The number of coupons redeemed can give you some insight into the relative importance of each directory to you. Third, they can be used to help a caller decide to call you instead of an advertiser that does not offer a coupon. Fourth, they can be a great closing tool during a sales call. Most of your Yellow Pages callers will not have taken the time to look at or cut out the coupon. This means you can use the coupon as an additional offer to attempt to close your sale. This works especially well when the purchase is rather sizable, like a water conditioner, a new roof, or a computer.

I would be remiss if I did not give you some additional guidelines for effectively using coupons. First, it is better to offer a specific dollar amount as a discount rather than a percentage. This helps you control the exact amount of the discount you are willing to give, and it tells the user exactly how much of a discount will be given. A coupon for $10 becomes a ten dollar bill and a coupon for $100 becomes a hundred dollar bill. Second, use multiple offers. You want the coupon to appeal to as many people as possible. Since different people are considering buying different things from you, multiple offers can increase the number of coupons used. Third, measure the overall impact of the offers by asking yourself how you would feel if ten times as many people as you expected redeemed them. If your answer is you wouldn't be happy giving that much away to that many people, you will want to change your offer accordingly. Finally, display the fact that you have a coupon in all of your ads in the Yellow Pages. The more important the coupon is to your business, the more prominent you want the coupon notification to be in your ad(s).

There are many other types of discount plans. Some Yellow Pages sales representatives will be more skilled than others at presenting them. Since you want to buy as skillfully as possible, you must make sure you get the information you need to evaluate the plans. If you are an existing advertiser, the first thing you want to know is what it will cost you to renew your existing advertising. The second thing you want to know is the rate increase over last year. Third, you want to know the percentage of discount are you receiving and the total discount in dollars. Fourth, if you were to buy certain specific ads, you want to know what your bill would be, what percentage of discount you would receive, and the total dollar value of the discounts.

When you have the answers to these questions, preferably in some sort of a chart or other written form, you can truly see what you are getting for your money. You can see when you are buying at a discount, to what extent you are buying at a discount, and the total value of the advertising compared to the price you will be paying. These simple steps will make you a much better buyer of Yellow Pages, and you will feel better about your purchase regardless of your decision. Even if you do not buy at a discount, you will know what you could have gotten by spending more and why you decided it wasn't the right buy for you at that time.

SAMPLE MARKETING PLANS

The following examples involve three different advertisers and various marketing plans. They will serve to illustrate the thinking that is involved in the buying process and why it is helpful to evaluate your options in a graphic format.

The first example is a real estate company with a 3/16-page ad in the current issue of a directory. The company is currently paying $274 per month for the ad. The ad was bought last year on a 50% discount offered to buyers of new display ads by the publisher. Option 1 in Figure 1 shows what it will cost to renew the ad for the next issue. As you can see, some of the discount is eliminated the second year. As a result, the client would pay $91 more per month to renew the program. The discount on the display ad would then be 33%. In addition, the publisher offers a free one-inch ad under another heading if the existing ad is renewed. The total value of the free space would be $262.25 per month.

Option 2 in Figure 1 shows what would happen if this advertiser doubled the size of his ad under the heading REAL ESTATE. In this case, the discount on the display ad would be approximately 34%. The publisher would give a free two-inch ad with this program. This option would mean an increase of $450 per month. The result would be that both ads would be twice the size of the current ad. While the amount of free space would not double, the publisher gives almost one dollar of additional discounted space for every dollar spent by the client for the space.

HEADING	OPTION 1 - RENEWAL AD SIZE	RATE	VALUE
REAL ESTATE	3/16 PAGE	$365.00	$548.00
REAL ESTATE-COMMERCIAL & INDUSTRIAL	ONE-INCH	$0.00	$79.25
REAL ESTATE MANAGEMENT	FREE LISTING	$0.00	$0.00
TOTALS		$365.00	$627.25
CURRENT BILLING		$274.00	
INCREASE		$91.00	
TOTAL DISCOUNTS			$262.25
HEADING	OPTION 2 - 3/8 PAGE AD AD SIZE	RATE	VALUE
REAL ESTATE	3/8 PAGE	$724.00	$1,030.00
REAL ESTATE-COMMERCIAL & INDUSTRIAL	TWO INCH	$0.00	$154.50
REAL ESTATE MANAGEMENT	FREE LISTING	$0.00	$0.00
TOTALS		$724.00	$1,184.50
INCREASE		$450.00	
TOTAL DISCOUNTS			$460.50

FIGURE 1

In this simple example, the decision will be based upon the value of doubling the size of the ad. In either case, the client will get a good buy for the money and will be buying at a substantial discount. In both cases, the client would be buying the display ad on a step-up program for next year.

Figures 2 and 3 illustrate options available to an advertiser from two publishers in the same market. Option 1 in Figure 2 shows what would happen if the client were to renew two existing half-page ads. This publisher would give the advertiser a free one-inch ad, a free 3/32-page ad, and a free coupon for renewing the ads. This option represents an increase of $297 per month over last year. The client had been paying full rate for one of the half-page ads and the other was on a step-up program. Next year, half of the step-up discount will disappear. That is the main cause of the increase in the cost of this program. You can also see that the client would receive $665 per month in free space. This total program would have a discount of approximately 20%.

Option 2 in Figure 2 considers increasing one of the ads to a three-quarter-page ad. This would result in an increase of $682 per month over last year, and one ad would be 50% larger. Both of the large display ads

HEADING	OPTION 1 - RENEWAL AD SIZE	RATE	VALUE
COMPUTERS - CABLE INSTALLATION	ONE-INCH	$0.00	$82.25
COMPUTERS - DEALERS	ANCHOR BOLD	$28.50	$28.50
COMPUTERS - DEALERS	1/2 PAGE	$1,245.50	$1,422.00
COMPUTERS - SERVICE & REPAIR	ANCHOR LISTING	$0.00	$0.00
COMPUTERS - SERVICE & REPAIR	1/2 PAGE	$1,422.00	$1,422.00
COMPUTERS - SOFTWARE & SERVICES	3/32 PAGE	$0.00	$285.00
COMPUTERS - SOFTWARE & SERVICES	ANCHOR LISTING	$0.00	$0.00
COUPON SECTION	COUPON	$0.00	$121.25
COMPUTERS-SYSTEM DESIGNERS & CONS	2 EXTRA LINES	$22.50	$22.50
TOTALS		$2,718.50	$3,383.50
CURRENT BILLING		$2,421.50	
INCREASE		$297.00	
TOTAL DISCOUNTS			$665.00

HEADING	OPTION 2 - 3/4 PAGE & 1/2 PAGE ADS AD SIZE	RATE	VALUE
COMPUTERS - CABLE INSTALLATION	ONE-INCH O		$82.25
COMPUTERS - DEALERS	ANCHOR BOLD	$0.00	$28.50
COMPUTERS - DEALERS	1/2 PAGE	$1,245.50	$1,422.00
COMPUTERS - SERVICE & REPAIR	ANCHOR LISTING	$0.00	$0.00
COMPUTERS - SERVICE & REPAIR	3/4 PAGE	$1,785.50	$2,149.00
COMPUTERS - SOFTWARE & SERVICES	3/32 PAGE	$0.00	$285.00
COMPUTERS - SOFTWARE & SERVICES	ANCHOR LISTING	$0.00	$0.00
COUPON SECTION	COUPON	$0.00	$121.25
COMPUTERS-SYSTEM DESIGNERS & CONS	2 EXTRA LINES	$22.50	$22.50
COMPUTERS -TRAINING	3/32 PAGE	$50.00	$285.00
TOTALS		$3,103.50	$4,395.50
INCREASE		$682.00	
TOTAL DISCOUNTS			$1,292.00

HEADING	OPTION 3 - 2 1/2 PAGE ADS W/COLOR AD SIZE	RATE	VALUE
COMPUTERS - CABLE INSTALLATION	ONE-INCH O		$82.25
COMPUTERS - DEALERS	ANCHOR LISTING	$0.00	$0.00
COMPUTERS - DEALERS	1/2 PAGE COLOR	$1,714.50	$2,070.00
COMPUTERS - SERVICE & REPAIR	ANCHOR LISTING	$0.00	$0.00
COMPUTERS - SERVICE & REPAIR	1//2 PAGE COLOR	$1,714.50	$2,070.00
COMPUTERS - SOFTWARE & SERVICES	3/32 PAGE COLOR	$0.00	$376.00
COMPUTERS - SOFTWARE & SERVICES	ANCHOR LISTING	$0.00	$0.00
COUPON SECTION	COUPON	$0.00	$121.25
COMPUTERS-SYSTEM DESIGNERS & CONS	2 EXTRA LINES	$22.50	$22.50
COMPUTERS -TRAINING	3/32 PAGE COLOR	$0.00	$376.00
TOTALS		$3,451.50	$5,118.00
INCREASE		$1,030.00	
TOTAL DISCOUNTS			$1,666.50

FIGURE 2

would be bought at a discount. The one-inch ad, the 3/32-page ad, and the coupon would still be free. In addition, another 3/32-page ad would cost $50 per month versus its full value of $285 per month. The total amount of free space would be worth $1,292 per month. In this example, by spending $385 more per month than a renewal would cost, the client would pick up an additional $627 per month in discounts. This total program would have a discount of approximately 30%.

Option 3 on Figure 2 illustrates what would happen if the client were to add one color to the two existing half-page ads. Both of the half-page ads would be bought on a step-up program. The one-inch ad and the coupon would still be free. In this case, the client would get two free 3/32-page color ads as well. This would increase the cost of the program by $1,030 per month and would result in total discounts of $1,666.50 per month. The discount for this program would be approximately 33%.

The trade-off here is clear. If the client chose Option 2, the decision would be based upon getting 50% more space under one of the headings and probably a better, more aggressive position under that heading. If the client chose Option 3, the decision would be based on the value of adding color rather than size. While the discounts would be greater with Option 3, I would recommend Option 2.

Figure 3 illustrates the differences that exist between publishers in the same market. This publisher gives dollars in the form of a discount as an incentive to close early rather than giving free ads. The client has a variety of ads and listings, some of which are also at a discount and some of which are at full rate. The two main ads are a half page and a quarter page. Both of the ads were bought on a step-up program last year. About half of that discount will go away the second year. The overall result is an increase of $334.25 per month and total discounts of $855.50 per month. The discount would therefore be approximately 30%.

Option 2 considers buying two half-page ads. In this case, the publisher offers a free ad when you pay full price for an ad of the same size. As you can see, by paying $221.75 per month more for the half-page ad under COMPUTERS—SERVICE & REPAIR, the client gets a free half page under COMPUTERS—DEALERS worth $1,478.75 per month. This

Chapter 6 • Buying Strategies

HEADING	OPTION 1 - RENEWAL AD SIZE	RATE	VALUE
COMPUTERS - CABLE INSTALLATION	BOLD WITH 2 EL'S	$49.50	$49.50
COMPUTERS - DEALERS	ANCHOR LISTING	$12.25	$12.25
COMPUTERS - DEALERS	1/4 PAGE	$609.00	$716.25
COMPUTERS - SERVICE & REPAIR	ANCHOR LISTING	$12.25	$12.25
COMPUTERS - SERVICE & REPAIR	1/2 PAGE	$1,257.00	$1,478.75
COMPUTERS - SOFTWARE & SERVICES	1/8 PAGE	$305.00	$358.75
COMPUTERS - SOFTWARE & SERVICES	ANCHOR LISTING	$12.25	$12.25
COMPUTERS - TRAINING	FREE LISTING	$0.00	$0.00
COUPON SECTION	COUPON	$83.75	$167.25
COMPUTERS - NETWORK	1 1/2 INCH	$90.00	$120.00
SUB-TOTALS		$2,431.00	$2,927.25
LESS EARLY CLOSE DISCOUNT		($358.75)	
TOTALS		$2,072.25	$2,927.75
INCREASE		$334.25	
TOTAL DISCOUNTS			$855.50
HEADING	OPTION 2 - TWO 1/2 PAGE ADS AD SIZE	RATE	VALUE
COMPUTERS - CABLE INSTALLATION	1 1/2 INCH	$60.00	$120.00
COMPUTERS - DEALERS	ANCHOR LISTING	$12.25	$12.25
COMPUTERS - DEALERS	1/2 PAGE	$0.00	$1,478.75
COMPUTERS - SERVICE & REPAIR	ANCHOR LISTING	$12.25	$12.25
COMPUTERS - SERVICE & REPAIR	1/2 PAGE	$1,478.75	$1,478.75
COMPUTERS - SOFTWARE & SERVICES	1/8 PAGE	$305.00	$358.75
COMPUTERS - SOFTWARE & SERVICES	ANCHOR LISTING	$12.25	$12.25
COMPUTERS - TRAINING	BOLD LISTING	$25.00	$49.50
COUPON SECTION	COUPON	$0.00	$167.25
COMPUTERS - NETWORK	1 1/2 INCH RED	$83.50	$167.00
SUB-TOTALS		$1,989.00	$3,856.75
LESS EARLY CLOSE DISCOUNT		($180.00)	
TOTALS		$1,809.00	$3,856.75
INCREASE		$71.00	
TOTAL DISCOUNTS			$2,047.75
HEADING	OPTION 3 - 3/4 PAGE & 1/2 PAGE ADS AD SIZE	RATE	VALUE
COMPUTERS - CABLE INSTALLATION	1 1/2 INCH	$60.00	$120.00
COMPUTERS - DEALERS	ANCHOR LISTING	$12.25	$12.25
COMPUTERS - DEALERS	1/2 PAGE	$0.00	$1,478.75
COMPUTERS - SERVICE & REPAIR	ANCHOR LISTING	$12.25	$12.25
COMPUTERS - SERVICE & REPAIR	3/4 PAGE	$2,092.75	$2,092.75
COMPUTERS - SOFTWARE & SERVICES	1/8 PAGE	$305.00	$358.75
COMPUTERS - SOFTWARE & SERVICES	ANCHOR LISTING	$12.25	$12.25
COMPUTERS - TRAINING	FREE LISTING	$0.00	$0.00
COUPON SECTION	COUPON	$0.00	$167.25
COMPUTERS - NETWORK	1 1/2 INCH RED	$83.50	$167.00
SUB-TOTALS		$2,578.00	$4,421.25
LESS EARLY CLOSE DISCOUNT		($358.75)	
TOTALS		$2,219.25	$4,421.25
INCREASE		$481.25	
TOTAL DISCOUNTS			$2,202.00

FIGURE 3

publisher offers an early close discount based upon the total amount of display space purchased. The result in the example is that the discount is reduced, but this is a buy that can't be refused when compared to a straight renewal of the advertising as shown in Option 1. For $71 per month more than the client is currently spending, the total discounts on this program go to $2,047.75 per month. Although it may seem almost unbelievable, the discount is approximately 53%!

The third option in Figure 3 is provided for comparison purposes should the client want to consider an even more aggressive move. In this case, the main ads would be a three-quarter page and a half page. Should the client pay full rate for the three-quarter-page ad, the half-page ad would still be free. Another option would be to buy the three-quarter-page and the half-page ads on the step-up program, but that would be a much more expensive way to buy the same space. In this option, the result would be $410.25 more per month than Option 2, but the discounts would only increase by $154.25 per month. This is still an incredible buy with approximately a 50% discount. Here the decision would be based upon the need for the larger ad under COMPUTERS—SERVICE & REPAIR.

Assuming this particular publisher offers the same discount program next year, the three-quarter-page ad could be a good choice for next year. If the client buys Option 2 this year, the free half page will be billed at 25% of full rate next year. If the client were to then exercise Option 3, the half-page ad would once again be free.

Frequently there is a lot of emotion involved in Yellow Pages buying decisions. Sometimes there are conflicting uses for the money. Small business owners sometimes even get their business money mixed up with their personal money. They think that if they spend a certain amount of money for Yellow Pages advertising, they will have less money to pay the mortgage or other personal expenses. When I encounter such thinking, I relate the following true story.

A young couple, just out of college, decided to open a lawn ornament business in Florida in the late 1970s. As soon as they opened their company, it was like somebody turned the water off. No one seemed to be buying lawn ornaments anymore. Their business was really hurting when they were approached by a plant salesman who offered to sell them plants on consignment. They were very tempted but hesitated because the owner of a nursery located two blocks away had sent them several of the few customers he had to date. The couple didn't think it would be right to compete against the owner of the nursery.

Fortunately, they discussed the situation with a business advisor and indicated their hesitancy to compete with someone who had been so nice to them. The business advisor gave them one of the best pieces of advice I have ever heard. He said, "Nonsense. You do what is best for the business!"

That is how the best Yellow Pages decisions are made. Ask yourself, "Is this going to be good for the business?" You may be afraid to buy Yellow Pages advertising. It may be something you don't want to do or something somebody else doesn't want you to do. You may not want to do it because you don't like the publisher of the directory or the sales representative. Personal opinions and feelings can get in the way of making a good decision. The bottom line is either the business will profit from the ad you are considering or it won't. If the ad won't increase your profitability, you probably shouldn't buy it. Conversely, if you need or want more business, that's what Yellow Pages advertising is intended to do for you.

The Yellow Pages buying decision is often potentially one of the most important business decisions made by business owners and professionals every year. Few of those for whom Yellow Pages advertising can make a significant contribution give the decision the consideration it deserves. Most decisions are based upon what I call the buyer's "comfort level." Most business owners and professionals have a spending limit which if exceeded would make them uncomfortable. In my experience, the limit may vary by type of business or profession, but it also varies considerably among people in the same business and the same marketplace. In fact, people tell you what their current comfort level is by the amount of representation they do or do not have in the Yellow Pages.

I found there was a direct correlation between how much someone was willing to spend and the profit gained from their efforts. Many of my customers needed me to influence their "comfort level" by pushing them to make a decision they were resisting making. I found the customers who appreciated me the most this year were the ones I had pushed the most last year.

In a sense, you are my customer as you read this book. I encourage you to try some of my recommendations to see for yourself if they work. I also encourage you to raise your "comfort level." The higher your "comfort level," the better Yellow Pages strategy you can put in place. The higher your "comfort level," the more total dollars of discounted space you will buy and the more you will get for your money in terms of both cost and income. Finally, I encourage you to give your Yellow Pages buying decisions the time they deserve in order to make a better buy for yourself.

7

AD DESIGN TO GET ATTENTION

This chapter will introduce you to the basics of ad design. In Chapter 8 we will cover copy content, and in Chapter 9 we will put the two chapters together and look at the final layouts. The appearance of an ad is a very personal subject. What you may think is very good someone else may think is terrible and someone else may think is acceptable. Let me set the stage by telling you I will make statements you may not agree with for various reasons. The important point is for you to realize that there are some basic truths that will help you advertise more effectively.

Once you have decided on the size of an ad, it is important that you truly understand how to make that ad work best for you. All ads of the same size under the same heading will not produce the same results. There is no one reason why this is true. Many factors determine the results of an ad. One reason you see such differences in ad design and content is not all advertisers agree on what is effective and what is not.

Obviously, an ad cannot be effective if it is not read. It must be seen in order to be read. An ad that stands out more will be seen more and, therefore, read more. That is one of the major advantages of larger ads. The larger an ad is, the harder it is for someone to not notice it.

Listings can be considered to be ads, but I won't devote much space to them in this book. For the most part, there are only so many things you can do to a listing to make it stand out more. One is to pay to have it set in bolder and/or larger type or, in some directories, set in color. You can also add copy between your name and address. Such lines are called extra lines. There is usually a limit to the number of lines you can use in this way, but obviously the more lines you add, the more attention your listing will draw.

Examples of this appear on page Y-9 in The Yellow Pages Sampler. The first listing under CATERERS for A Fine Affair is probably a free listing. The listing for Atwood's Family Buffet stands out more because it is in bold type. The listing for Danny's Open Pit Bar-B-Que stands out even more because it is larger still. In addition, two extra lines of copy have been inserted between the name and address for Danny's, which gives more information and at the same time increases the space taken up by the listing.

To gain even more attention with an in-column ad, you can purchase what is called a space listing. These ads can be as small as a half-inch and as large as a four-inch ad in most directories. Several examples of these ads appear on pages Y-10 and Y-11.

The in-column ad on page Y-10 for Mars Catering is a one-inch space listing. Space listings are surrounded by a thin-line box and are quite restricted in terms of type style and the use of attention-getters in the ad. Usually no illustration is allowed in a one-inch ad, so the only thing that may be available to draw more attention to it would be the addition of color.

You can see what the addition of color and the purchase of a slightly larger ad does for Nature's Finest Catering on page Y-10. This is a one-and-one-half-inch ad. Obviously, there is room for more copy. Certainly

Chapter 7 • Ad Design to Get Attention

the addition of color helps this ad as well. I like the use of color in small ads such as this because the total dollar cost per month to add color is relatively small, yet the pulling power of the ad is enhanced.

On page Y-11, you will see two larger in-column ads. These are three-inch space listings. Some art is allowed in ads such as these. The restrictions on art vary by publisher. The increased size coupled with the use of some art helps to draw attention to Ribs & More Bar-B-Q's ad. The use of art and color for Sheridan Plaza Hotel's ad adds to its attention-getting capabilities compared to the other in-column ads and listings.

When in-column ads are competing with display ads under a heading, the display ads usually win in their ability to draw your eye. More art can be used, better art can be used, different borders can be used, and larger space can be purchased. Also, contiguous display ads help each other to distract the eye from the listings and in-column ads. Take some time to browse through The Yellow Pages Sampler and study the in-column ads. You will see that some are more effective than others of the same size. Some use art better than others and some use color better than others. You can find similar examples of good and bad in-column ads in your own local directories and on page Y-32 in The Yellow Pages Sampler.

Display ads are intended to allow you to attempt to attract as much attention as possible. There are far fewer restrictions on overall design and the use of various type styles. Because display ads can be more complicated and because there are more things you can do with them, the rest of this chapter is devoted to guidelines for creating display ads.

On page Y-32, you will see four small display ads for Dean Brothers, Inc. If you look through your local directory, you will find ads like the first example for Dean Brothers at the far left. When you compare the first ad to the second ad, which has a much bolder border, you have to ask yourself why someone would place an ad like the first one when it costs no more to add the bold border. It is obvious what the simple addition of a more eye-catching border can do.

Most publishers allow a great deal of freedom in the use of borders. In the case of Dean Brothers, even the overall shape of the ad has been changed just by rounding the corners and getting away from the boxy look of the first example. Travel through The Yellow Pages Sampler with me as I make some comments about what we see in terms of borders.

On page Y-3, the border for Markham Flooring's ad not only has a different shape, but its design is tied into the type of business. On page Y-4, the ad for BC Interior Design Center in effect is one big border. On page Y-5, the merging of WJC for Wayne Jones Carpet is another variation of a border to help differentiate the ad from others on the same spread-page.

Page Y-6 shows an example where I believe the advertiser has gotten too clever. Notice that there is no border around the ad for Elegant Flooring. Couple this with the small telephone numbers in the ad, and a user could conceivably call the ad below for Paul's Rug Showcase, thinking they were one ad.

On page Y-7, the design of the border for Quality Flooring & Tile's ad takes up too much of the total ad space. This is the second smallest display ad you can buy, and in this case almost 25% of the space is devoted to the illustration used as the top portion of the border. When you read Chapter 8 on copy, you will learn why this is not good use of space. Certainly in this case, the ad is only competing with one slightly larger display ad. The need for attention is not nearly as strong as it would be if there were a half dozen or more competing ads on this spread-page.

The ads for Rolling Along Bar-B-Q and Manning's Cafe & Grill on page Y-9 utilize an irregular border design effectively by opening up a portion of the border. Big Bear Catering on page Y-10 does this in another way. The problem in this case is similar to the problem with the border design in the ad for Quality Flooring on page Y-7. Only two-thirds of the space in this ad is dedicated to information about the business, including its address and telephone number.

On page Y-15, the full-page ad for Rooter Service of Ft. Smith has a border that does almost nothing to draw any additional attention to the ad. Obviously, the designer of this ad believes in the white space principle of advertising, which will be addressed in Chapter 8. For now, it is sufficient to note that this border does nothing to enhance the attention-getting quality of the ad.

The ad for C. Hammer Plumbing on page Y-16 is a somewhat unique way of bordering an ad and giving information at the same time. On page Y-17, the best that can be said about the border around Farragut Plumbing's ad is it does segment the copy and make it easier to read than if a straight rectangular border had been used.

The ad for France Plumbing on page Y-19 is another example of how to make the entire ad a border. I particularly like the use of a great deal of solid black in the ad. Solid black will be discussed again later in this chapter.

Aztec Plumbing again has a rather creative border design on page Y-21. While C Hammer's ad on the same page may be somewhat creative in its design, the overall result is little room for information in the ad. As you continue looking through The Yellow Pages Sampler, you will see other examples of both good use and almost totally ineffective use of borders.

Obviously, good illustrations and artwork can add to the eye appeal of a display ad. One of the most common attention-getters is the use of line drawings. There are three types of line drawings: simple line drawings, detailed line drawings, and line drawings that use some form of a screen. An example of a simple line drawing is the faucet in the R L Williams Plumbing ad on page Y-22. The faucet in Panel Plumbing's ad on the same page has more detail to it and as a result looks more realistic. On page Y-21, the faucet in Aztec Plumbing's ad shows the use of screening, which gives the illustration more depth.

I generally recommend detailed line drawings with the use of screening over photographs. You always know how a drawing is going to look, unless you reduce it too much. (The more detail a drawing contains, the "muddier" it will look if it is reduced too much.)

There are several problems with photographs. When you photograph a building, there may be things in the photograph, such as cars in front of the building or telephone poles, that can detract from the appearance of the building. Sometimes trees will add shadows to the picture, which can also detract from the appearance of the building.

Generally speaking, you never know how a photograph is going to print in a Yellow Pages ad. The original photo may look great, but for some reason it can turn out much lighter or much darker when it appears in the ad. Some of this has to do with the reduction of the photo when it is placed within an ad and some of it has to do with the printing process used for many Yellow Pages directories. In any case, it is better to stay away from the use of photos as much as possible. Since this book is not printed on the same presses or paper as a Yellow Pages directory, I cannot give you examples of what happens to photographs. However, if you look in your local Yellow Pages, you will undoubtedly find examples of poor reproductions of photographs that take away from the total image of the ads.

This can be especially true of photographs of people. Frequently, attorneys, doctors, and other professionals like to use their own photograph or a photograph of their staff in their ads. A good photograph can make a good professional impression (although we have all seen poor photographs and wondered why the people would want to use them). At the same time, an unflattering photo or one that is too dark or too light can detract from the image of the ad. In some cases, the photo may looked fine on the proof from the publisher but is much too dark or too light when the ad appears in the directory.

A few tips can improve the look of photographs. Frequently, it is not the object or person in the photograph that is the problem but rather the background in the photograph. If the background is too light and the object or person in the foreground is also rather light, the whole photo can look faded. If the background is too dark and the object or person in the foreground is very dark, everything seems to run together in one dark image. One solution to prevent either of these situations is to crop the photograph. If you are using a photo of a building or person, have the printer remove the background and just use the outline of the building or person. This eliminates the possibility of the background being the problem.

Make the photograph as large as practical in the ad. Because the original photograph will be reduced in most cases, some of the detail will be lost in the reduction and some distortion of shading will result because everything will be closer together.

Some publishers simply do a better job of printing ads with photographs. Take a look at the directory you are considering. Examine ads that contain photographs. If the majority are clear and look good, you can expect similar results if you provide the publisher with a good quality photograph. If you see a lot of poorly reproduced photos, be forewarned that you will be playing Russian roulette if you use a photo in your ad.

One case where you need not be wary of using a photo in an ad is if the publisher utilizes process color. This process does an excellent job of reproducing color photographs in ads. In fact, in a process color ad, the use of a photograph is preferable to the use of a line drawing, if possible. The reproduction is that sharp and the effect is that great.

As mentioned, one use of screening is in a line drawing. There are other ways to use screening in an ad as well. Most publishers have three basic screens available: a 30% screen, a 50% screen, and a solid screen. Without getting into unnecessary technicalities about the screens, they appear as light grey, dark grey, or solid black when printed in black ink. In color, the shading goes from light to medium to solid.

The shading behind the truck in Carpets On The Go's ad on page Y-2 is a graduated screen effect. This can be quite effective and is being used more and more in ads. In the ad for Discounted Flooring Systems on the same page, the company name is in a solid black screen. The letters are called reverse on solid black. This can be an effective way to make certain parts of an ad stand out. You will find many examples of this throughout The Yellow Pages Sampler and in your local directories as well.

This leads us to the discussion of color. Today, almost all Yellow Pages directories offer at least one form of color. When color was originally added to Yellow Pages, the only color that was available was red. Today, many publishers have red, green, and blue available, as well as the use of all three colors in a process called spot color. More and more publishers are adding process color, which gives them the capability to reproduce almost any color in the spectrum.

It is obvious that the use of color can be an attention-getter. The use of color also adds a premium to the cost of an ad. There are times when it is appropriate to consider buying color and there are times when it is not. Some general guidelines for the use of color follow:

1 The smaller the ad, the more you should consider using color. The additional monthly cost to put color in a one-inch ad, for example, is very small. The ability of color to draw attention is very obvious, if it is done right.

2 Use as much color as possible in the ad. Take a look at the ad for Printer's Alley on page Y-28. What does the use of red do for this ad? It has probably added 30% to the cost of the ad. Perhaps the buyer of the ad does not like red and feels too much use of it would look cheap. He could have bought green in this directory for the same price. It is the upper left-hand half of this ad that draws your attention to it. Would it have been even more effective if it was solid green instead of black? As this page is made up, perhaps so. The buyer of this ad either should have saved some money and not bought red at all or should have used whatever color he bought to a much greater extent than he used red.

The same considerations apply to the two-inch red ad for Gordon Plumbing Company on page Y-19. The buyer is paying for red, yet less than half of the space in the ad uses it. The advertiser is trying to compete with much larger ads on this page, and the use of color helps. If the entire body copy of the ad had been set in red, it certainly would have stood out even more and would not have cost one cent more.

3 Whatever color you buy, use a great deal of it in solid shades. The ad for Panel Plumbing on page Y-22 uses a light shade of blue in the center part of the ad. If this had been done in solid blue with reverse type for the copy, the ad would jump out at you even more than it does.

4 Buy color at a discount whenever possible. If you have a black ad in a directory, sometimes it will cost you very little to add color. These programs are explained in more detail in Chapter 6—Buying Strategies. When you can buy color for one year at almost no additional cost, do it.

5 Beware when your sales representative says he or she will give you color for free. The major Yellow Pages publishers have written marketing plans that determine the price of every ad in every situation. In some of these plans, a color ad bought at a discount is the same price or almost the same price as the same ad without color bought at full price. Be sure to find out if you can buy the black ad at a discount as well, in which case you would not be getting a particularly good buy on color. You have a right to know whether you can buy either ad at a discount. If you think color is worth it, fine; if you don't, you should not be misled into thinking it is free. If you follow the basic guidelines for evaluating discounts given in Chapter 6, you will know exactly what you are paying for color.

6 You can frequently buy an ad that is 25 to 50% larger for about the same money you would pay to add color. This affects the position of your ad as well as the amount of space you have to tell your story. The only exception to this is when you are considering adding color to the largest ad available under the heading.

It is important to emphasize that ad design is a very personal subject. Few ads take full advantage of the tools available to get attention. This is reflected in the simple small display ads for Dean Brothers at the bottom of page Y-32 in The Yellow Pages Sampler. All four layouts say exactly the same things, but two of them obviously do it much better. The only question is whether or not to use color to attract even more attention.

8

COPY: HITTING THEM BETWEEN THE EYES!

In addition to domination, copy is another factor that determines what size ad to purchase. While size helps to get the user's attention, it is the information contained within the ad that determines the ultimate success or failure of the ad. What is the Yellow Pages? It is an information medium. Its users expect to find the information they need to help them decide where to buy. It only makes sense that if you do not give prospective buyers the right information about your company, you risk not getting their calls. Because different customers have different needs, your ad should appeal to as many of those needs as possible if it is going to be as effective as possible. It is critical that you understand this point and keep it in mind when preparing your ad.

Many an advertiser seems to think that a clean ad is an effective ad. This thinking is probably based on what is known as "the white space principle." The problem is the white space principle stems from studies of newspaper readers. This is like comparing apples with oranges. Yellow Pages usage occurs when the user is ready to buy something. This is not nearly as frequently the case with a newspaper reader, whose main purpose is to read the articles in the newspaper. Something must distract the reader from the line after line of type in a newspaper article. White space in a newspaper ad serves this purpose.

There are, of course, times when the ads are of great interest, but newspapers primarily attract readers with news and features. That puts a limit on how much time someone is usually willing to spend reading a newspaper ad. Therefore, brevity is probably a good attribute for a newspaper display ad.

An exception to this is the classified section of the newspaper. The reader of the classified section, like the Yellow Pages user, is looking for buying information, not editorial content. Is an automobile dealer's classified newspaper ad more effective when it just contains a slogan and the name, address, and telephone number of the company? Or is it more effective when it gives the prices of particular cars the dealer has on sale this week? Car shoppers who use the classified section want and expect to find the latter. The dealer's slogan is of relatively little importance to them.

Just as excessive white space and the lack of buying information do not work in the classifieds, they do not work in the Yellow Pages either if you are trying to attract new customers who know little or nothing about you. Advertisers will argue this point more strongly than almost any other aspect of Yellow Pages ads other than the relative importance of size. Before you make up your mind, consider the following.

Usage is "the process of elimination." It is also "the process of selection." Ads that are not seen are eliminated. Ads that do not state that they have or do what the user wants are eliminated. Ads for businesses that are not conveniently located for the user are eliminated. Ads for businesses that are not open when the user needs them to be open are eliminated. As "the process of elimination" progresses, the result eventually is "the process of selection."

This process is really quite simple. It is easier to select a business if you know from its message that it has what you need when you need it and where you need it. Since different users need different things, an effective ad hits as many of them "between the eyes" as possible. In most cases, this cannot be accomplished in just a few words, just as a sales presentation that is too brief and lacks sufficient information for the buyer to make a decision cannot be effective. In other words, if most businesses hired sales representatives who said as little about their companies as their Yellow Pages ads do, most of the sales representatives would be fired!

But all copy is not created equal. Some words are just words and do little to help the results of an ad. Other words are extremely powerful and can greatly influence the results. The most powerful words in most Yellow Pages ads are the location of the business. This can be so powerful that Yellow Pages publishers have created mock directories with fictitious locations to test the value of size and color in terms of the effectiveness of an ad.

Why is the location factor so strong? Let's assume you and I offer the same products and services and most of our customers come to our locations. I am in the far north end of the directory distribution area, and 10% of the population covered by the directory is within five miles of my location. You are located in the center of the distribution area, and 50% of the population is within five miles of your location. Which ad will produce the most results? Let's take this example one step further. Suppose I have one location within five miles of 10% of the population and you have four locations within five miles of 80% of the population. How much more effective would your ad be?

Just how important is the location factor? The following little-known secret to increasing Yellow Pages results should answer that question. The explanation is a bit involved, so bear with me.

It is possible to increase the results of an ad merely by adding telephone numbers from surrounding communities. To some degree, the more telephone numbers, the more calls. The law of diminishing returns potentially can set in, but few advertisers ever approach that situation. This approach works for businesses whose customers come to them as well as for businesses that go to their customers.

Let's start with an example where the customer comes to you. Suppose you own an automobile insurance agency and have one location. Most of your business typically comes from within a very small radius. If you were to add telephone numbers and community names from the surrounding vicinity, you would increase the number of calls from those communities. A second number will not double your calls and a third will not triple them. However, if the communities are large enough, the increase in calls will more than justify the cost of the additional telephone lines. Some of the people in the surrounding communities could just as easily do business with you as with a competitor located in their community. Some may work near your location or live on the side of town close to your location in the adjoining community. The closer you appear to be to them, the more likely you are to get their calls. To some people, your location can be indicated by your telephone exchange.

The location factor is achieved through the use of a service known as a Remote Call Forwarded Telephone Number. Most telephone companies have them. With a remote call forwarded number, you can get a telephone number from literally any community and the call will be forwarded to your location when someone dials the number. The telephone company usually charges a small per-minute fee for the calls in addition to the monthly charge for the line. The calls are metered, and the telephone company tells you the volume of calls you received.

With this information, you can evaluate the response to the new number in your ad on a monthly basis. But there is more that you can do with this information. You can also use the new number as a form of a market test. Let's assume that you would consider adding a location in a community if the demand were great enough. Metering gives you an idea of the potential demand for a new location. You will lose some of the calls because you are not physically located in the community in which you are advertising, but you might be surprised by the number of people who will be glad to come to your location if it is to their benefit. If you add one or two more numbers from other communities to your ad, you can compare the relative drawing power of the various proposed locations. This is a good way to help your businesses grow. First, you can increase the response to your ad. Second, you can identify strong potential new locations and eliminate locations where there is less interest in your product or service.

It is important not to advertise these numbers in any other medium. You are trying to increase the response to your ad and measure the results at the same time. You can also use this technique to totally meter your ad. You simply get another remote call forwarded number from the community in which you are located and have it forwarded to your main number. Take the main number out of your ad (the remote number will still ring at your location), and the result is a totally metered ad. You can increase the number of calls by adding numbers, market test the communities served by the numbers, and measure the volume of calls from your ad all at the same time.

This tactic works just as well for businesses that go to their customers, as many service businesses do. For some reason, many of us prefer to do business with a service company in our area rather than one located on the other side of the county or in another county. Your telephone number indicates your location to some degree. This can help you and it can hurt you. If you get one or more remote call forwarded numbers from strategically located communities, you can expand the sphere of influence of your ad. You will get more calls, and you will do more business from those calls.

Suppose you would like to serve some communities in an area covered by an adjoining directory. If you run an ad in that directory using your main telephone number, you will get some calls. You will also fail to get some calls if your ad does not have a local telephone number for those communities. This is especially true if prospective customers have to make a long-distance call. If you use a number(s) local to the communities you are trying to serve, responses will increase. As in the previous example, this strategy can also help you determine if the area is worth considering as an additional location for your company.

Some areas of the country show a great understanding of the multiple telephone number strategy, and others show almost no understanding at all. Look in your local directories under headings such as PLUMBING

CONTRACTORS and LOCKS & LOCKSMITHS. If you see multiple numbers being used in the largest ads, your market is aware of the pulling power of additional telephone numbers. If you don't see this to any great extent, you have an edge over your competition when you employ this strategy.

Just as location and telephone numbers are important, so is certain specific information about your products and services. You know what you sell and you know how much of it you sell. You have a good feel for the relative demand for all of the products and services you handle. The more important a product or service is to your business or practice, the more important it is to devote space to it in your ad. The greater the importance, the greater the space you should devote to it.

Brand names are extremely important. This applies to both sales and service businesses. If someone wants to buy a certain brand of a product and your ad says you sell it, you have a better chance of getting that sale than a competitor who doesn't say he or she sells it. This is especially true if you service more products than you sell. The phrase "service on all makes" is a lazy attempt to get a specific user to call. It also is an ill-informed attempt. A user who knows nothing more than he or she has a Ruud air conditioner is more likely to call you if your ad says that you service Ruud. This works so well in the air conditioning business that some knowing contractors include Honeywell in their list of brands serviced even though Honeywell does not make air conditioners. Honeywell makes thermostats. Some homeowners think that is the brand of their air conditioning unit because Honeywell is the name they see on the thermostat. And that is the brand they look for when they need service.

Other information can also be extremely important in the selection process. Hours of operation are important to someone using the directory after what is generally considered to be normal business hours. In a retail business, these are the hours the business is open, but in a service business it could be the availability of twenty-four-hour service seven days a week.

I recommend you conduct a copy study to determine what you should and should not say in your ad. Make a list of all the copy points stated in the ads under the heading you are considering. Once you compile this list, you can eliminate the things your competitors are saying that you either don't want to or can't say. What you are left with is a list of things you probably want to say. This gives you the foundation on which to build the content of your ad.

I have done such a study for the PLUMBING CONTRACTORS heading on pages Y-14 through Y-25 of The Yellow Pages Sampler. I found a total of 102 copy points just in the display ads under this heading. Some copy points are similar to others, but there were at least 102 different ways to make statements about plumbing businesses. It is interesting to note what some of the ads say and others do not. For example, repiping a house is a big job for a service plumber. It usually costs thousands of dollars per job, yet only half of the twenty-two display ads mention repiping. Similarly, detecting hidden leaks is another rather expensive job. Yet only two of the ads use the words "leak detection." You can probably find similar situations under the heading you are considering.

Another interesting finding in the copy study is the number of copy points per ad. Of the three full-page ads under the PLUMBING CONTRACTORS heading, one has thirty-one copy points, another has twenty, and the third has ten. There are four third-page ads. One has thirty-five copy points, two have twenty-one, and the fourth has nineteen. Of the five half-page ads, one has twenty-seven copy points, one has twenty-three, one has twenty, one has nineteen, and one has eight. Would you expect the same results from two ads if one gives over three times as much information as the other? If we were analyzing small, relatively inexpensive ads, the lack of copy might a little easier to understand, but these are half-page ads and larger in a metropolitan directory.

The results from either a full-page ad with ten copy points or a half-page ad with eight copy points can be increased dramatically just by adding good, quality information. It is that simple!

Study your heading(s). See what your competitors are saying about their businesses. Compare those statements with what you know your potential customers want and need. Look for the missing copy points in your ad.

Identify those points you want to include in your ad. If you take the time to do a copy study, you will be way ahead of much of your competition. The more aware you are of the importance of copy content, the more you will see that most advertisers do not give this vital element of Yellow Pages advertising the attention it deserves.

9

PUTTING YOUR AD TOGETHER

You have bought an ad that is large enough to draw attention to it. You have designed your ad so that it draws attention in relation to competing ads around it. You have filled your ad with as much useful information as you can. You now have the ingredients for a successful Yellow Pages ad. And you are way ahead of most of your competitors because they probably have not taken the time to do all that you have done in preparing your ad. Some of your competitors may be hard to compete with in other advertising mediums and other marketing activities, but most of them are relatively easy pickings when it comes to competing with them in Yellow Pages.

There are a lot of reasons why your competitors' efforts are not as good as you might expect. Part of it has to do with misconceptions about Yellow Pages advertising in general. Part of it has to do with misconceptions about the importance of copy. Part of it is because other pressing responsibilities come first, which means that Yellow Pages decisions are often rushed. Part of it is because not all Yellow Pages sales representatives educate their customers to the degree they should. Part of it is because some Yellow Pages advertisers just doesn't care. Part of it is because many Yellow Pages advertisers simply dislike the whole process of buying Yellow Pages advertising.

All of the above factors give you a true competitive advantage. This chapter is devoted to the finishing touches you can put on your efforts to make them even more effective. You have selected the illustration(s) you want to use in your ad. You have decided whether or not to use color in your ad. You have identified the copy points for your ad. Now you are ready to have your ad put in its final form.

Ideally, you will do this with the help of your Yellow Pages representative and hopefully not at the last minute. The more time you allow for this process, the better the odds of having an ad you will be proud of and that will be effective for you. After you give the guts of your ad to your Yellow Pages representative, the publisher prepares a sample layout of the ad with all of the pieces put together.

You are now looking at two things: the attention-getting ability of your ad and the readability of the contents. We have discussed the ingredients that can draw attention to an ad. Certainly the use of a good illustration(s) is important in this regard. There are basically two types of illustrations: those that have great eye-catching power but really don't say much about the business and those that both draw attention and give information.

An example of the former would be a line drawing of a man scratching his head, with a question mark at the top. The headline might read, "Wondering Where To Rent It?" If the illustration is well done, it might draw attention to an ad for a rental store. Compare that to an ad with line drawings of six trailers and trucks with the size indicated under each drawing. If this illustration is well done, it would draw attention to an ad for a trailer and truck rental business and at the same time give the reader information about sizes available. In addition, the advertiser's enhanced awareness of the use of illustrations in Yellow Pages would be rewarded by the fact that some callers would refer to specific sizes shown in the ad. Illustrations that give information about the business or practice are preferable.

Next, you should determine the most important selling point in the ad. This can be taken from your list of copy points. You want to prioritize them so you can decide what you want to emphasize and what you just want to mention. Give your prioritized copy to your Yellow Pages representative as a guide for the artist doing the layout for your ad. Preferably, the most important copy point should be used as a headline.

"But," you may ask, "shouldn't my name be at the top of ad?" The answer is sometimes, but only sometimes. The more successful your business, the more important the name can be. Someone using the Yellow Pages without a particular name in mind may choose your business because your name is familiar. In addition, the more successful your business is, the more the references to your heading will be from users looking for you. These are just two reasons why your name should be prominent in your ad if you are a well-known business. But that does not necessarily mean your name has to be at the top of the ad in order for it to be easily seen.

Most Yellow Pages advertisers want to attract new customers or clients. Most of these customers are not looking for you in particular, but they are looking for something. The right headline can help convince them to call you. Look at your list of copy points. What is the single most important point you can convey to the kinds of customers you want to draw from the ad? That should be used in your headline.

Notice the differences in the four layouts for Dean Brothers, Inc. at the bottom of page Y-32 of The Yellow Pages Sampler. Doesn't the headline Free Delivery Available help to sell Dean Brothers better than when Dean Brothers, Inc. is used as the headline? Now look at the examples on pages Y-30 and Y-31. Don't the headline Fast, Courteous Service and the subheadline American & Imports—Cars—Trucks—RV's sell better than the name T.G.D.? In fact, if you look at the display ads throughout The Yellow Pages Sampler, you will find most of the advertisers did not understand this important difference. Remember, these pages are based on real directories. What they represent is a lack of understanding on the part of most of the advertisers and a lack of effort on the part of the Yellow Pages sales force to guide their customers.

One headline I have used through the years for a variety of businesses has never failed: Rush Orders Don't Upset Us! My most recent use of this headline was for a florist. It has become the key statement in all of this florist's advertising. It is effective because it appeals to the last-minute buyer. It works for the advertiser because price is less of a consideration to the last-minute buyer. Therefore, this headline generally brings a high-quality purchase as opposed to someone just looking for the best price. It works for printers, formal wear rental stores, and movers, to name a few.

Once you decide on the headline for your ad (whether it be your name or a true headline), you can start to organize the rest of your message. The examples for Dean Brothers, Inc. on page Y-32 show how the same information can be organized in different ways. Notice how the copy has been segmented, especially in the third and fourth examples. Segmenting makes it easier to read the ad because it puts the copy into logical pieces. Each piece is directed toward either every reader of the ad or those readers interested in a specific product or service.

Some layouts have a more logical flow to them than others. The four ads on pages Y-2 and Y-3 are good examples. The ad for Carpets On The Go on page Y-2 is disorganized. The result is that it is easy to skip over or miss a copy point such as Free Shop-At-Home Mobile Showroom Service. The ad for Discounted Flooring Systems reads much better from top to bottom and left to right. The problem with this ad is that it could have given a lot more information and still have been very readable. The copy in the middle of the ad could have been expanded to include brand names and other important information and still not have looked too cluttered.

Markham Flooring's ad on Y-3 is another example of a disorganized layout. Compare that to the logical presentation of information in the ad for Nick's Floor Coverings. Also compare the information content in Nick's ad with the lack of similar content in Discounted Flooring Systems' ad.

There are different ways to segment copy logically and effectively. One is to use different type styles and sizes. The quarter-page ad for Chef Tom's Catering on page Y-9 illustrates this. Each section of the copy is separated from the others merely by using different type styles and sizes. The result is a neat, easy-to-read presentation of the information.

The quarter-page ad in red for Rolling Along Bar-B-Q & Catering on the same page adds the use of screens to further separate the copy points. You can see the contrast it creates and the various effects of the use of a lighter screen versus the use of a solid screen. Again, this is a logical presentation with good separation of information.

Another example of the use of a solid screen is the ad for Manning's on the same page. Full Service Catering and the telephone number jump out of this ad. Imagine the difference in the overall message if Fresh Seafood were to replace Full Service Catering in the reverse strip. The target market would have become more specific and the nature of the calls would change.

Another way to segment copy points is by the use of color. The ad for C. Hammer Plumbing on page Y-16 illustrates how color can do this. The ad for Conway Plumbing on page Y-18 also does this. The Yellow Pages Sampler also includes some examples of the use of color to segment copy in in-column ads. It is preferable to make full use of color in such ads to get full value for the cost of the color. When you buy an in-column ad with color, you can segment copy by varying type styles used in the ad.

Segmentation can also be achieved by the overall design of the ad. BC Interior Design Center, Inc. on page Y-4 has a layout that accomplishes segmentation in this manner. The problem with BC's ad is the name, address, and telephone number take up far too much space. However, it is a very readable ad for the content it does contain and it is a good overall design. Better examples of this type of segmentation are the display ads on pages Y-17 and Y-19. Both are well done without devoting too much space to a small amount of the total information given in the ad.

You may not agree with every comment made in this chapter because, as mentioned previously, your impression of the appearance of an ad is based on personal taste. No layout is perfect. Someone can always find at least one thing to criticize in any layout. Your ad should be the right size, say the right things, and be readable. Quality and quantity of copy are paramount. Your ad should convey what you want people to know about your business, and you should be pleased with the presentation. After all, it is your company that is being represented and your money that is paying for the advertising.

10

THE SALES REPRESENTATIVE: FRIEND OR FOE?

I came very close to never selling Yellow Pages advertising. In the 1960s, Yellow Pages representatives were considered to be strong, aggressive salespeople, frequently too aggressive. Some might even have been described as "slick." I never thought of myself as that kind of person, and I had no intention of working for a company that expected me to sell that way. But an employment agency counselor convinced me to at least interview for the job. I found the Reuben H. Donnelley Corporation was going through a change in philosophy at the time in an effort to become more customer-focused in their selling approach. And the rest is history!

Yellow Pages sales representatives are like all salespeople—some are good and some are not so good. As a general rule, they are salespeople and not order takers. This is not the kind of a sales position where an order-taking approach would work very well. The position provides the opportunity to make an above average living, and Yellow Pages publishers look for individuals with good basic selling skills and/or experience.

Yellow Pages sales training is among the finest sales training given by any organization in this country. The job is quite unique as sales positions go. The sales representative must sell almost any kind of business or profession imaginable on the merits of Yellow Pages advertising. This is not an easy task. Each business owner or professional thinks his or her business or profession is unique and, therefore, relates better to a sales representative who understands that business or profession. There are significant differences among types of businesses and professions. There are different customer bases and marketing approaches. There is much to be learned to understand this wide range of customers.

A good Yellow Pages sales representative will, over time, become very knowledgeable about his or her directories, the markets they serve, and what I call "the common threads of business." There are certain secrets to operating a successful business or professional practice. It is not just a matter of being good at what you do or offering the best price on what you sell. Success means the ability to attract the amount and type of customers or clients needed to make the business or practice profitable. Some businesses need a lot of small customers whereas others need a few big customers, but most need a combination of both to survive and thrive. The nature of the Yellow Pages sales position is such that representatives can get a common-sense degree in successful business practices. They see what creates success and what causes failure because they see both every day—if they keep their eyes open.

Not every Yellow Pages sales representative who calls on you is going to be that knowledgeable about your business. It would be nice if they all were, but everyone has to start someplace. At one time, even you were not nearly as knowledgeable about your business and your customers as you are now. The important trait you are looking for is whether or not the sales representative knows his or her product. Can he or she help you make a better buy?

I can't think of another product where sales representatives get such mixed reactions from their customers. One of the difficulties in selling Yellow Pages advertising is that most customers tell their sales representatives that Yellow Pages are not as effective as the representatives have been told in their training. If it weren't for the relatively few customers who have a very positive opinion of the effectiveness of Yellow Pages advertising, it would be an impossible job to sell the product ethically and honestly. If you are someone who has doubted the value of Yellow Pages, understand that you are in the majority. Over time, sales representatives who hang in there discover the differences in perspective are caused by the differences in results, and the differences in results are caused by the differences in effort on the part of the advertisers.

Every Yellow Pages representative should be able to provide certain things to you no matter how long he or she has been on the job. They all have demographic information available to them about the markets they cover. They can usually give you population figures, number of automobiles, number of households, and per capita income figures. They can tell you when, where, and how many directories they deliver. They can quote rates for specific ads and tell you what discounts are available. They usually have national and local usage studies about Yellow Pages in general and about their specific directory. If they cannot give you an answer to a specific question, they should be able to get an answer for you.

What you are looking for is a degree of customer orientation on the part of your sales representative. The more sincere interest the representative shows in you and your business, the more you can trust him or her to do extra things for you. You can tell when someone is more interested in making a sale than in benefiting you. The less customer-focused your representative is, the more you are going to have to work to make sure that lack of focus does not keep you from profiting from your Yellow Pages advertising.

Personalities are involved in the Yellow Pages buying process. Since I started buying Yellow Pages instead of selling them, I have a much better understanding of some of the resistance shown by Yellow Pages advertisers toward Yellow Pages sales representatives. Some Yellow Pages representatives make it easy to buy from them and some make it very difficult. Since my job is to produce results, I can't let personality differences get in the way of doing my job to the best of my ability. And neither can you.

It is easy to tell you what to do when you have a really good representative. You let the representative help you. The question is what do you do when you have a representative who is not that helpful and concerned with your welfare. You have to keep in mind the potential importance of what you are doing in buying Yellow Pages. You are trying to produce profitable income. In the long run, it is the advertising you buy, and not the quality of the Yellow Pages representative, that determines the profitability. If your representative is less helpful than you would like, you need to take charge and make sure you get what you need.

So what can you expect? You can expect help with the layout and design of your ads. Yellow Pages publishers employ artists to produce proposed layouts called spec copy. You should make use of this service to ensure that you get an effective ad for your money. We have already discussed guidelines for the design and content of your ads. Now you want to make sure you are happy with the finished product. It is not your job to produce that finished product. It is the job of the publisher to provide you with the finished product.

Most publishers provide proofs of display ads before publication. This requires some cooperation on your part. It is much easier to provide a proof to an advertiser who places an ad well in advance of the closing date of a directory than it is when the advertiser places an ad during the final days of the sales campaign. As a result, publishers that offer proofs have proof close dates. If you submit your ad before that date, you will usually get a proof for final review. The earlier you place the ad before the proof close date, the more time you have to review the ad and the better your chance of being able to make last-minute changes. The era of laptop computers has improved this whole process, and it won't be long before you will be able to get a proof on the spot when you place an ad with some publishers.

The last thing you want to be is rushed in the buying process. The larger the directory you are considering buying, the longer the selling time for that directory. Some of the more rural directories may have campaigns that last only a few weeks. The less time the sales representative has to get the job done, the more rushed the rep will be. If you let your representative know you are willing to work in the early part of the sales campaign, you will find the representative much easier to work with than you probably would be at the end of the campaign.

Many Yellow Pages publishers segment their advertisers based upon the amount of money the advertisers spend with them. They usually assign their better, more experienced representatives to their larger advertisers. This means the more you spend, the better your chance of getting an experienced representative. It also means that if you increase your advertising substantially, you may qualify for one of the more experienced representatives in the future. Generally speaking, these representatives are more knowledgeable and, hopefully, more customer focused.

One of the potentially most important tools a sales representative has is called a heading book. There are thousands of headings available in Yellow Pages directories. No representative or advertiser can know all of them. These headings are constantly changing because of constant changes in products and services being offered. Most major publishers design their heading books to give headings related to other headings. It is not unusual to find out about a new heading from the list of related headings. Suppose you are in the garage door business and have always advertised under the heading DOORS. Some publishers have now added the heading GARAGE DOORS & OPENERS. This is an important change because many users probably looked under the G's when they needed this type of business, only to discover no such heading existed. In the past, they have had to rethink their decision and try D for doors. As publishers add this new heading, users can find what they want under the G's. If you are in the garage door business, you want to know about this new heading.

When cellular telephones first came into use, the advertising for this service was placed under MOBILE TELEPHONE EQUIPMENT & SUPPLIES. The heading CELLULAR TELEPHONE EQUIPMENT & SUPPLIES was only added in the last few years. Now that it is available, it is an obvious choice for businesses that sell this equipment.

Make your Yellow Pages representatives work for their money. Let them make suggestions and discuss their product with you. You need good local information to help you make the best buying decisions. If you find your representative lacking in product knowledge, ask to see his or her sales manager. If you are dissatisfied with your sales representative, ask for a replacement. You have a right to expect and receive good service and advice.

You have the ability to make your sales representatives better or worse. If you are cooperative, that will be reflected in your representative's attitude toward you and your business. After all, sales reps are only human. Some of their customers treat them better than others, just as some of your customers are easier to deal with than others. Even the poorest of Yellow Pages representatives will perform better with a little respect and cooperation.

One final comment. There is another type of Yellow Pages sales representative that you should know about. There are people in the Yellow Pages industry who call themselves Yellow Pages consultants. Their main focus is to show you how to "save" money. They position themselves as experts who will give you the straight story about Yellow Pages.

These consultants are even more commissioned than your Yellow Pages sales representative. They receive a percentage of the money they "save" you. The result is their incentive is to "save" you as much money as they can. Their sales pitch is an easy one. They just tell you want you want to hear: You don't have to spend all that money in Yellow Pages.

These consultants hurt many more businesses than they help. The truth is most of the advertisers the consultants approach are not spending as much as they should to truly benefit the most from their Yellow Pages advertising. Like all professions, there are some very good Yellow Pages consultants who approach their clients in a constructive manner. Should you be approached by a consultant, just be aware of how the consultant makes his or her money and the motive for telling you what he or she does.

11
MAKING THE ADVERTISING WORK

As mentioned previously, Yellow Pages advertising does not create sales; it creates leads. It can do its job and still not be profitable, or as profitable, as it should be. Profitability is determined by how the leads are received and handled. Sales are the life blood of any business. Too frequently, leads are literally "headed off at the pass" before they have a chance to be turned into sales.

Twenty-five years ago, it bothered me when I would call an advertiser and no one answered the telephone. What if I were a potential customer? What would I think? What would I do next? Would this company have lost my business? There really weren't too many alternatives if a business owner wasn't available to answer the telephone back then.

Unanswered telephones are not much of a problem anymore. Today, we have answering machines, answering services, and even voice mail to do the job when someone from the business is not available to answer the telephone. All of these methods are a definite improvement over an unanswered telephone. They get calls for a business that the business would not get without them. That is the good news.

The bad news is they are overused, abused, and lose calls that would not be lost if someone from the business answered the telephone. Each way of answering the telephone serves a purpose at the right time and in the right place, but all three lose business as well as keep business from being lost.

An answering machine is better than an unanswered telephone, and that is the extent of it. If someone calls and truly needs to talk with you, chances are they will leave a message on your machine. But if the person doesn't know you and needs to talk to someone now, there is a good chance they will just hang up and call someone else when they get your answering machine. What a waste! If an average call produces $20 worth of business for you, it doesn't take many hang-ups before you lose a significant amount of income. If your average call is worth $50, $100, or more, the loss is even more serious.

An answering machine is the method of last resort for receiving calls. If your customers seldom call you after business hours, an answering machine may suffice. However, when a customer would reasonably expect to be able to reach you, it is not a good alternative.

Some business owners do not feel they can afford an answering service. In some cases, an answering machine can be a stop-gap measure until a better solution is found. But there are right ways and there are wrong ways to use an answering machine. The wrong way is to record a message that merely states you are not in and will return the call if the caller will leave a message. You haven't told your callers anything that will encourage them to leave a message. They don't know when you will return or when they can expect to receive a call from you.

If you have to use an answering machine, try making a new recording each time you leave. Tell the caller what day it is and what time of day you left. Tell the caller when you will return and when they can expect to receive a call from you. This may seem like a lot of extra bother, but it works. More new customers will leave a message in response to your message than would ever respond to a vague "Hi, I'm not in."

Even if you use the more detailed type of message, the answering machine will still lose business for you. If you are in a service business, like carpet cleaning or plumbing, you will lose over half the calls that are generated by your Yellow Pages advertising. What a waste! You did what you had to do to get those calls when you bought the advertising but negatively affected the results of the ad(s) by using an answering machine.

A carpet cleaner with whom I worked for several years had the largest and first ad under his heading. Each year he would tell me how much business he got from his ad and quote his ratio of sales to the cost of his ad. One year when I went to see him, he said, "Tom, I'm not getting half the business from my ad this year that I have gotten in the past. You know how well I keep records and the numbers don't lie."

Something didn't make sense. He still had the largest and first ad. He was in a growing area, so there was almost definitely more business in his market. There wasn't an unusual increase in the competition under his heading. Through experience, I had learned that when something unexplainable like this happens, it is usually a telephone answering problem.

I asked him if anything had changed in the way he was answering his telephone. He told me he had gotten rid of his secretary and was now using an answering service to take his calls when he was out of the office. He told me the name of the answering service; it was one of the best in town. Despite this, I told him the answering service was the problem. He disagreed and said they were very good at what they did.

I finally convinced him to bring a secretary in one day a week. He then compared the average number of sales leads he received per day with the secretary to the average per day with the answering service. Several weeks later, he hired the secretary full time. His results were twice as good with her than without her. She could answer questions about the business that the operators at the answering service couldn't. She could quote prices. She could schedule appointments. She could close sales over the telephone. The result was she produced twice the business for him as the answering service. The other way to look at it is that the answering service lost half of the potential business on the calls they answered.

Answering services are a step above an answering machine, but sometimes only a small step. They certainly are more expensive than an answering machine, so it is important that you use a good one and that you see to it they answer your calls in the best way possible.

If you must use an answering service, you want them to sound like someone in your office and not like an answering service. They should answer the telephone with the name of your company followed by a phrase such as "Tom speaking." They should avoid saying they are the answering service unless the caller asks. They should indicate they will either be hearing from you shortly or they can reach you right away and you will call the caller right back. The advent of beepers has been a great help in this regard.

If you use an answering service, recognize its limitations and use it only as a last resort or at a time of day when it can hurt you the least. Like an answering machine, if someone really needs or wants to talk to you, they will leave a message with the answering service. If someone could just as well try to do business with a competitor, the answering service may well lose that call for you.

Voice mail is not much better than an answering machine and certainly not as efficient as an answering service. It is hard to believe that large companies that would not think of using an answering machine use voice mail to receive calls during normal business hours. It may be acceptable for non-sales departments to some degree, but it is not really effective for sales and marketing departments.

All of these substitutes for the real thing can affect the results of your Yellow Pages advertising. You have worked hard to get good quality leads from your ads, only to leave them lying on the ground, worthless, because you failed to capture them through poor response to the calls you received. If you or your staff cannot be there to take the calls, an answering service is preferable to an answering machine and an answering services in combination with a beeper is better still.

In the early 1980s, a new alternative was developed: call forwarding. No longer do you need to have an extension of your line at an answering service. You can now forward and un-forward your calls to an answering service as you see fit. More than that, you can forward your calls to someone whom you have taught to answer your telephone the way it would be answered by someone in your office. This is a great interim step for someone who opens an office but can't afford to keep it staffed full time during normal business hours. With proper training, such an individual can outperform an answering service and have a batting average closer to that of a full-time employee.

The mid to late 1980s brought an even better tool: the cellular telephone. Better still is the portable, hand-held cellular telephone. It can be the small businessperson's best friend in helping to build a business. A business is built on individual sales. The person most capable of making those sales for a small business is usually the owner. But the owner is sometimes the whole company. How can the business be built quickly if the owner is losing leads because he or she is busy away from the place of business? In the past, this owner had little choice but to use an answering service or an answering machine.

Today, those calls can go with the owner. Calls can be forwarded from the business telephone to a cellular telephone that goes anywhere the owner goes. A portable, hand-held instrument makes it possible to be by the telephone at all times. Sometimes the calls may come at inconvenient times, but if it means getting business you would lose otherwise, it is worth it.

The cellular telephone can be the small business owner's most valuable tool. If more small business owners did the amount of advertising they should do in the Yellow Pages (and elsewhere) and used a cellular telephone to capture the leads, they would build their businesses a lot faster.

We are about to enter the age of the single telephone number that will follow you wherever you go. That will make it even easier to build a business because fewer leads will be lost.

The last critical point in the advertising cycle is what happens to a lead that comes to your company. At this point, sales ability and interest in making the sale are of major importance. Think about your own experiences as a buyer. Think about how you have been treated by companies you considered doing business with. If you were to contact four businesses, they would not all be equal in terms of getting the information you needed. Some would know their business better. Some would be more concerned with you, the customer. Some would be cheaper and some more expensive. In the end, one would get your business and the rest would not.

How good are you and your people at handling leads? How responsive are you to your customers' needs? These are important questions. If you are good, you can improve. Only you know how well you perform in this area, which has a major effect on the success of your Yellow Pages advertising or any other advertising you do.

How do you feel about callers who price shop? Do you dislike talking to someone who is only interested in the cheapest price? Most people probably have at least some negative reaction to the so-called price shopper. If all buyers always bought at the cheapest price, most companies would be out of business. Somewhere in the course of a sales conversation the subject of price will come up, unless the buyer already knows the price. Price shoppers are like most Yellow Pages customers. They will usually pay less unless they are convinced they will benefit by paying more.

This chapter is not intended to be a sales course. The purpose is to point out how important you are to the success of your Yellow Pages advertising. Once you place your ad, it will produce the number of leads it will produce. That number cannot be changed. What can be changed is your success ratio in converting those leads into sales. That is the bottom line. If you are twice as effective as a competitor that has the same size ad, you have made your ad more effective for you. The more you spend on advertising, the more you stand to make or the more you risk losing.

Most local telephone companies offer some type of training or information on the subject of turning telephone inquiries into sales. See what your local telephone company has to offer. This service is usually free. It can only make you and your people more effective in the long run.

12
TYING IT ALL TOGETHER

Some very simple, key truths have been presented in the preceding chapters. The most important ones are the importance of dominance, the importance of an ad full of information, the use of multiple telephone numbers in an ad, and the strategy of multiple ads for certain advertisers. In this chapter, all the pieces are tied together in a story about five businesses. Their identities will not be revealed, and I will speak in some generalities where I could give you some specifics. The point is it is a true story that reflects the significance of these key truths.

Each of the five businesses had a full-page ad in the same directory under the same heading. Two of the businesses had common ownership and had multiple locations. Two others also had multiple locations. The fifth business had a single location. All five were in a business that gets good results from Yellow Pages advertising.

In a single year, three of the five full-page ads were canceled. The business that owned two of the ads canceled one and consolidated its two businesses in its remaining full-page ad. The owner of one of the other multiple-location businesses canceled because he no longer was willing to buy a full-page ad in both of the competing directories in his market. The third full-page ad was canceled by the owner of the other multiple-location business. Although he had built an important part of his existing business through the years from Yellow Pages advertising, he decided he no longer saw value in continuing the full-page ad.

The owner of the two full-page ads kept the first ad under the heading. The three ads that were canceled were the second, third, and fourth ads under the heading. Therefore, the owner of the fifth ad moved up to the second ad under his very competitive heading the next year. This had a significant effect on the results from his advertising.

The owner of this single-location business used remote call forwarded numbers to measure the results of his advertising. In addition, he listed additional telephone numbers in his ad to increase the calls from the ad. As a result, he was able to measure the effect the change in position under the heading had on the results from his ad. Before going into those results, let's talk a little more about the experiences of this business and the results the owner achieved from Yellow Pages advertising.

This advertiser has done some interesting things with the content of his full-page ad over the years. As he has added specific copy points, he has seen specific results. Each of these changes was made in separate years, so he was able to see the effect of each one as it happened.

One of the changes he made was to add copy directed toward a specific segment of his market—the high end of his potential customer base. He devoted approximately 15% of the space in his ad to telling these customers he had what they needed. When the new issue of the directory was published, he immediately saw an increase in calls from this particular type of customer. This segment of his market became an extremely important part of the results he achieved from his ad, and the profitability of the ad increased dramatically with this copy change.

In a subsequent year, he added another copy point directed toward newcomers to his market. Many of these newcomers find they need something he offers when they buy another product. This causes some of them to refer to Yellow Pages to find someone who can provide this service. The year he added this copy point (and it only consists of four words), he again saw direct results from the addition. As of this writing, only one of his competitors mentions this service. He just scratches his head and wonders why his competitors can't see what is obviously working for him.

The last copy point he added was aimed at offering discounts to specific customers. The nature of his business is such that some customers qualify for additional discounts on their purchases. He now makes these customers aware that these discounts exist, and his calls for the discounts have increased accordingly.

He also uses multiple telephone numbers in his ad. For several years, he used three numbers, all of which were remote call forwarded numbers. Therefore, his entire ad was metered. He could tell from year to year just how many calls he was receiving. The year he added a fourth number to the ad, his total calls increased by approximately 25%. With the four telephone numbers, he can also evaluate which of the surrounding areas are producing the highest volume of calls.

He added the fourth telephone number the same year he moved from the fifth ad to the second ad under his heading. Obviously, he didn't know he was going to move up this fast. He added the fourth number almost in desperation. Even though he had purchased the full-page ad for several years, he really was considering reducing it that particular year. The cost of the ad was one of the biggest "expenses" he had. He thought he would improve his cash flow if he reduced that expense.

He was having a difficult time as a single-location business competing with many multiple-location businesses. That made his full-page ad much more costly per location than the cost per location of his competitors' ads. The use of multiple telephone numbers helped to increase his calls, but it couldn't totally compensate for the lack of multiple locations.

He decided not to reduce his ad that year. And thank goodness he didn't! The volume of calls to the three telephone numbers when his ad was fifth under his heading increased by 50% when his ad moved to second under his heading. In addition, his fourth number produced so many additional calls that his total calls almost *doubled* in one year. What a difference this made in the profitability of his business. Imagine how glad he is that he didn't listen to the cost-cutting voice inside of him and chose to go after more revenue instead.

It takes courage to buy a full-page ad in Yellow Pages, especially when you are not a large, highly profitable business. Many business owners are not that brave. Those who are really make Yellow Pages advertising work for them.

If this owner had gone with his original instinct that year, he would have seriously affected his business in a negative way. He knows that now. He now knows even better how wrong many of his competitors are to focus on the "cost" of Yellow Pages advertising.

Let's not forget the other four businesses. How did their actions affect them?

The business that had two full-page ads must have discovered it was not a good move to cancel one of them. The following year, the owner again bought the second full-page ad. As of this writing, those businesses have two full-page ads plus an additional half-page ad under the same heading. The two businesses had relied upon Yellow Pages from their very inception. That one year, the owner focused on the cost aspect of the ad. After that year, it appears that he returned his focus to generating revenue.

The third multiple-location business has not bought another full-page ad in this directory, although it still has a full-page ad in the competing directory. From all indications, this business has not grown since the full-page ad was deleted. In fact, it has lost income since then. Other factors that had nothing to do with whether or not it was in the best interest of his business led this owner to his decision.

The fourth multiple-location business has continued with a relatively small ad in the directory since its full-page ad was canceled. For years, this owner focused more and more on the cost of his full-page ad. It probably was only a matter of time before he reduced the size of the ad. He listened to his people who answered the telephone. He asked them about the calls from Yellow Pages, and they told him what he wanted to hear (and probably what they thought he wanted to hear). They told him all he was getting was a bunch of price shoppers from the Yellow Pages and they were writing very few orders from these calls.

It turns out Yellow Pages was "the exception, not the rule" in the case of this business. Most of the business was built in other ways. All Yellow Pages did for this business over the years was make it more profitable than it had been before it drew from the Yellow Pages well. Like the owner of the other multiple-location business who has stayed with his decision, this owner probably still thinks he made the right decision. He is still in business, so it didn't ruin him. He certainly isn't wrestling with the cost of his ad anymore. He has no idea how many calls per month he has given up because he never cared enough to meter them.

If you were to talk to the business owners who have reduced their Yellow Pages ads, they would probably tell you they made the right decision. In fact, they would probably go into some detail as to why they made the right decision. In terms of their priorities, they did make the right decision. In terms of a profitable return from Yellow Pages, they made the wrong decision. They made a decision based upon the cost aspect of Yellow Pages. It is as if they have blinders on that keep them from seeing income from Yellow Pages. It is as if they only see the benefit of writing a smaller check to the publisher each year and can't (or won't) see the loss of revenue.

The star of this story was driven by income. The only thing that made him keep the full-page ad that year he so badly wanted to cancel it was the realization that he needed income from the ad. He knew a great deal of his customers originally came from his Yellow Pages ad. Competition had become tougher, and his income was affected by the increased competition. Yellow Pages results do not happen in a vacuum. Outside influences, good and bad, play a significant role in determining the profitability of the results. But this owner bought to drive income, which proved to be the right strategy for him.

One final point about size. This single-location business also has a display ad in a competing directory whose distribution and usage are comparable to the directory in which its full-page ad appears. This display ad is approximately one-sixth the size of the full-page ad. It also is metered, although it only lists one telephone number. It produces about one-eighth as many calls as the full-page ad. Who is determining the results from this effort—the publisher or the advertiser?

13
THE PAST, THE PRESENT, THE FUTURE

The Yellow Pages has truly come a long, long way. There is some argument concerning the first classified directory, but it is safe to say it did not exist until some time in the 1880s. Like most new developments, it was pretty simple in its original form. The first classified directory (which later became the Yellow Pages when it was printed on yellow paper instead of white) consisted of alphabetical listings under alphabetically arranged headings. It was nothing fancy because our needs were not very great and the demand for the product was limited at best.

Through the years, the Yellow Pages proved that there was a growing need for this information source as the United States grew as a country and as a marketplace. As the product gained acceptance and as telephone companies recognized it as a source of revenue, the Yellow Pages became an addition to virtually every telephone directory.

The coverage of a directory was quite simple. Telephone companies had business offices. Those offices were responsible for a group of telephone subscribers within certain geographical limits. For example, the Chicago directory was delivered to the telephone customers of the Chicago business office of the Illinois Bell Telephone Company. Each business office throughout the country had its own customers and provided its own telephone directory to those customers.

As the product developed as an information source and as a source of revenue for its publisher, the variety of ads available to the advertiser increased. Businesses started competing with each other for the attention of the Yellow Pages user. They found, or at least some of them found, that size could make a difference. They found they needed space to tell their story in an effort to convince the user to call them.

At the same time, the telephone companies found that certain headings were more productive than others. Businesses represented under the more productive headings were willing to spend more money for larger ads.

The growth was slow and gradual until the end of World War II. The U.S. economy and standard of living grew dramatically as we moved into the 1950s. The Yellow Pages started to reflect that growth as two-column directories were expanded to three columns and eventually some were expanded to four columns to accommodate the increased number of businesses and the increased size of their ads.

When I entered the industry in 1966, the Yellow Pages was at its peak in terms of acceptance. Yet that acceptance was still limited in terms of usage and advertiser acceptance. We were starting to become the mobile society we now are. We were just entering the beginning stages of the rapid changes in technology and lifestyle that we have seen since then. Those changes made the Yellow Pages change and forced at least some of the potential advertisers to realize what a profitable source of business the Yellow Pages had become.

In the 1960s, business owners generally believed few of their customers or potential customers needed to use the Yellow Pages to find them. They made Yellow Pages buying decisions based on the principle that everybody knew them. There was a great deal of truth to that statement, especially in small towns. But we were increasingly becoming a nation of consumers. New products were introduced constantly. Buying decisions became more complicated. The need for a handy buying reference grew with these changes. Yellow Pages usage grew as a result of and with these changes.

Today, we buy more products and services, and we buy them more frequently from businesses that are relatively unfamiliar to us. We have been born and raised on Yellow Pages, so to speak. The Yellow Pages is a much more important resource to us than it was to our parents. There are more businesses available to us, providing more products and services than ever before. It only makes sense that Yellow Pages would experience the tremendous growth that industry experienced in the 1970s and 1980s.

With that growth, some farsighted entrepreneurs saw an opportunity to create directories designed to compete with those published by the telephone companies. They started with what are known as neighborhood directories. They distributed their directories in a different way than the telephone companies did. They developed directories to cover specific market areas not recognized by the telephone companies. In some areas, especially the suburban areas, markets grew inside of larger directory coverage areas. The rates in these neighborhood directories were usually much lower because their distribution was less and more focused to serve a specific market.

Many of these directories failed. In most cases, the failure could be tied to a lack of acceptance and therefore a lack of usage. Some did succeed, and some of the pioneers still exist. But the industry was really turned upside down with the breakup of AT&T. With the breakup, telephone companies started to consider competing with each other in each other's directory markets. This change, coupled with the growth of non-telephone-company publishers, led to what we have seen since the breakup of AT&T—a proliferation in the number of telephone directories published.

Most homes and businesses today receive at least two directories from different publishers. In some markets, such as Southern California, people get three, four, and even five directories. Like most things, there is good and there is bad in this proliferation.

The good is the increased competition has caused some significant changes in the directory business. During the 1970s and well into the 1980s, a pattern of annual rate increases became established. In the real growth areas, these increases were frequently in double digits. These kinds of increases have almost ceased to exist today. The Yellow Pages industry is now a price-competitive industry. Obviously, this has been a beneficial change for directory advertisers.

Until the late 1980s, there were no deals available to the Yellow Pages advertiser in the majority of markets. This has changed drastically, as discussed in Chapter 6 on buying strategies. Today, most publishers offer marketing plans. Some of the weaker publishers will even deviate from their plans and offer even greater incentives if they want the business bad enough.

The Yellow Pages user has also benefited from the increased competition. Many publishers fill the front of their directories with all sorts of useful information, such as maps, local community events, zip code maps, and even audio information services which provide sports scores, stock market news, horoscopes, and a wide variety of other interesting information.

There is a down side to the increased competition as well. All of the original directories have been weakened at least to some extent by their new competition. Some of their usage has been taken from them, and the result is they are not the same buy they once were. I am not aware of any major directory that has had reduced advertising rates as it has lost usage to competition. The best that can be said is the rates are not raised as significantly as they were in the past.

The reduced growth in Yellow Pages revenues has caused directory publishers to become too product focused and not enough customer focused. They have become concerned with product differentiation, which is not necessarily the same as product improvement. There has been a rapid growth in color options, in-ad audio options, consumer buying tip sponsorships, and other additions to the product line of many publishers. These additions are focused on increasing revenues with the underlying hope they will also prove beneficial to the user and the advertiser.

Chapter 13 • The Past, The Present, The Future

Confusion abounds about the Yellow Pages today. The user can hardly tell one directory from another. Frankly, most users do not care whose directory they are using. They just want to find what they are looking for in the one they are using. But all directories are not created equal. Some have more "holes" in them than others. Some just do not contain as much information. The users do not understand why. They just expect to find what they want when they use a directory. When they can't, they become frustrated. To them, directories just are not as good as they used to be.

Advertisers not only become frustrated, they get angry. They did not ask to have more than one directory serving their market. Yet many of them are afraid not to advertise in a new directory that covers their area. In truth, they have created their own monster. If an advertising community does not support a new directory, the directory will cease to exist. It is that simple. So the advertiser complains and feeds the source of the complaint at the same time.

The most confusing thing is who the advertiser should believe. Usage figures given by competitive directories never match. In some markets, if you added the usage figures, you might get as much as 150% usage, which is impossible. So who is telling the truth and who is not? Is anybody telling the truth? This is the least attractive aspect of the Yellow Pages in its current state. The product is often misrepresented when it really does not have to be. All any advertiser has a right to expect is a reasonable return on the money spent for a Yellow Pages ad. The advertiser does not have a right to expect unrealistic returns and, at the same time, should not be led to believe they will be achieved.

The Yellow Pages industry has struggled with the changes that have occurred in recent years. It will continue to struggle, for even more drastic changes lie ahead. Print is going electronic; we all know that. The question is to what extent and how fast. The Yellow Pages industry should be able to deal with the future better in many ways than it has in the past. There is a lot about the future that is predictable. The breakup of AT&T and what it meant to the industry was not predictable.

So what is the future? Those directories that get the usage will continue to exist. Those that lose usage, and many will, will fail if the loss is significant. Yellow Pages survives on the retention of a high percentage of its advertiser base. That base is built upon a return on the investment in Yellow Pages, and the return is a result of usage—pure and simple.

The proliferation of printed Yellow Pages directories has probably reached its peak. There will always be someone trying to get a piece of the pie but, for the most part, this will be mainly in the area of more specialized directories, such as Spanish or other foreign language publications.

What will increase is the availability of electronic classified information. The telephone companies are trying to stay on the leading edge of this change because they know they will lose usage from their current directories to this information source in the future.

As existing directories lose usage, their advertiser support will dwindle as well. This does not mean the directory publishers will reduce their rates. That would be suicidal. It would mean advertisers willing to renew at higher rates would actually pay less, which would be like asking to take an unnecessary loss. What I believe will happen is a loss in size of ads. Full-page buyers will reduce their advertising to three-quarter-page or half-page ads. Half-page advertisers will reduce their advertising to quarter-page ads and so forth. It will be very difficult for publishers to maintain their current income let alone grow their printed product in this environment. This will force them to go with the user. If the user is going electronic, then directory publishers will have to go electronic to find growth.

Developing new product lines is essential to all companies, but the key will be how customer focused those new products are. The Yellow Pages experienced significant growth during the 1970s and 1980s because it was the right product at the right time. That was when we saw significant changes in the advertising of the legal and medical professions. They found the Yellow Pages to be an effective source of clients and patients. At the same time, users found the Yellow Pages a helpful reference as the crime rate, divorce rate, bankruptcy rate, and number of lawsuits increased. Add to this the increased medical coverage for a substantial portion of our population, coupled with the increased specialization in the medical profession, and the result was dramatic increases in the advertising under the legal and medical headings.

Now we have the new telecommunications bill. What will it mean? More companies will apparently be in the business of being our local telephone company. Will each of them publish a directory? Will the number of Yellow Pages publishers explode? What will the impact of the cable companies be as they enter the telephone industry? There are a lot of opinions. Mine is the strong will get stronger and it will be very difficult for the smaller players. They will have to rely on price to get their customers. Lower price will mean lower profit and probably inferior service. The telephone industry is a very capital-intensive industry. That means you need deep pockets to succeed.

The need for the buyer to find the seller will continue to be there. Change will continue to take place in technology and in how and what we buy. As a Yellow Pages advertiser, you will need to be alert to these changes. You will need to find efficient ways to monitor your results so you build a foundation for your future decisions.

Yellow Pages advertising may be a negative subject to many business owners, but that doesn't change the product, the usage it gets, or the amount of business it produces for its advertisers. Someone will get the business that flows through the Yellow Pages. A high percentage of that business will go to the relatively small percentage of advertisers who use the Yellow Pages effectively.

Yellow Pages advertising is not for everybody, but if you are in the right kind of business or profession, it has the potential to be more than just Yellow Pages. It has the potential to be Yellow Gold if you know how to mine it, now and in the future.

14 DISPELLING THE MYTHS

There are many myths about Yellow Pages advertising. This chapter will serve as a summary of some of the myths discussed in this book. They are all key points that bear repeating. In the introduction, we discussed opinions, how common they are, and how dangerous they can be. The most dangerous opinions are the myths about to be dispelled.

MYTH #1
BIG ADS CAUSE BUSINESSES TO FAIL

I certainly will not say that overbuying (or overselling) of Yellow Pages never occurs, because it has, it does, and it will. First, brand new companies seldom buy huge ads. In fact, most companies never in their entire business history ever buy as much as a quarter-page ad, let alone a half-page or a full-page ad.

Second, there is a period of time between the purchase of an ad and its publication date, a minimum of three months but as much as one year. Many things can and do happen during this period that probably have more to do with the failure of a business than a large Yellow Pages ad. Companies usually fail because of lack of business, not an overabundance of business. True, overbuying can contribute to the failure of a business, but usually the business is in a weakened state for other reasons. Seldom can Yellow Pages be given total credit for the success of a business and seldom can it rightfully be given total blame for the failure of a business.

Not buying enough Yellow Pages advertising contributes more frequently to the failure of a business than overbuying contributes to its demise. Then why do so many people believe Yellow Pages is a strong contributing factor to the failure of many businesses? It has to do with the nature of the product. It contains ads for most businesses that serve a market. Its life span of twelve months means that the failure of any business with an ad in the Yellow Pages will be reflected for all or some portion of that twelve-month period. The business fails but the ad is still present for all to see. This does not happen in most other mediums. A newspaper advertiser that fails, for example, ceases to appear in the newspaper, so the failure is not nearly so obvious.

All the Yellow Pages does, generally speaking, is provide leads. The sales have to be made by the company behind the ad. If the telephone is not answered, or is answered poorly, potential business is lost. Handling calls properly can have a major effect on the bottom-line results of your Yellow Pages advertising. Think about your own experiences in trying to do business with companies over the telephone. Many do a pretty sorry job in this area. Do they cause their Yellow Pages ads to fail?

MYTH #2
MANY OF THE MOST SUCCESSFUL BUSINESSES DON'T HAVE BIG ADS

This valid statement has less to do with the value of Yellow Pages than it does with the fact that there are many sources of revenue other than Yellow Pages advertising. Yellow Pages only represents a piece of the action. For some businesses, like moving companies, it can be a huge piece. For others, like furniture dealers, it represents a relatively small percentage of the total potential customer base.

Some very successful moving companies have relatively small Yellow Pages ads. These companies usually do not do a lot of business with individual families. Their contacts are through corporations and they do a lot of commercial and industrial moves. Government contracts are another source of business for some of these companies. While these companies are concentrating on getting business elsewhere, many of their competitors are literally taking business from right underneath their noses in the Yellow Pages.

Some businesses just don't want the customers they could get from the Yellow Pages. They have established a special niche for themselves that justifies the lack of a strong Yellow Pages presence. An example would be a printer that specializes in high-quality, high-volume printing work whose potential customer base is located in several states. The Yellow Pages is not the way most of this business is attained.

Some businesses literally cut off their nose to spite their face. Frequently they have had a bad experience, or a series of bad experiences, with Yellow Pages representatives and companies. If they get angry enough, they prove to the Yellow Pages representatives and themselves that they can succeed without a big ad in the Yellow Pages. That does not make their decision right; it just means there are other substantial sources of income to be utilized.

Another factor has to do with the size of a successful company. We usually equate success with sales volume. The larger a company, the less likely the buyer of Yellow Pages advertising for that company has any reliable feedback about Yellow Pages results that would be of great help in making the correct buying decision. Frequently the person making the buying decision in such a company cannot even be reached by Yellow Pages representatives to influence the buying decision. Opinions have been formed, and there is often considerable resistance to changing Yellow Pages policies within such companies. Large companies can usually make many times the profit from larger Yellow Pages ads that their smaller competitors can. The difference is their willingness to put the Yellow Pages into its proper perspective. If more large companies understood the value of Yellow Pages, the Yellow Pages would change drastically. By placing larger ads, they would have a significant effect on the results of the ads now placed by their smaller competitors and reduce the potential value of the Yellow Pages to those competitors. Many medium-size and smaller businesses succeed in the Yellow Pages because of the ignorance of their larger competitors who actually have a better buy in the first place because of their size.

Buying Yellow Pages advertising can be a tedious process. This is especially true when buying in more than one market. The situation is further complicated when multiple headings are involved in the decision. It becomes even more complicated when the markets are served by more than one publisher. The easy way out is not to take the time to evaluate each market, each heading, and each publisher. The easy way out is to simplify the decision-making process by establishing a standard representation for each heading without considering the market or the directory. This is the route taken by many large companies. Once such a decision is made, there is resistance to changing it because of the work involved in buying Yellow Pages in a more strategic and thoughtful manner.

MYTH #3
PEOPLE BUY BIG ADS TO FEED THEIR EGOS

Someone who buys an ad for ego purposes usually is not spending his or her own money. Some people in charge of advertising for a business like to brag about how big they are or how big they are going to be and spend a great deal of money in the Yellow Pages. That is easy to do when it is not your money. This does not happen frequently, but it does happen. When the buyer's money is on the line, the attitude is completely different. Even if the buyer is extremely successful, he or she is cautious about how the money is being spent.

You can't believe what everyone tells you about the size of their ad in the Yellow Pages. I have had many a customer tell me about the half-page ad they bought when, in fact, half-page ads were not even available at the time. In later years, this type of individual would talk about the full-page ad he or she had in a directory that did not offer full-page ads. Someone you may think bought a large ad to inflate his or her ego did not buy a large ad at all. The truth is much of it is empty talk.

MYTH #4
ONLY THE LARGEST ADS GET CALLS; SMALLER ADS ARE A WASTE OF MONEY

A letter on the subject of Yellow Pages put out by a franchise to its franchisees essentially conveyed this message. The letter was written by a marketing manager who had some strong opinions about the subject but very little knowledge. What a potentially damaging letter that was. Franchisees look to their franchiser for advice in areas where they feel deficient. If the franchiser says so, it must be right!

Such a statement fails to recognize that all pages have traffic. Therefore, all listings and ads get some calls; the largest ads definitely do not get all of the calls. If small ads did not work to some degree, especially under the most competitive headings, they would cease to exist. It is that simple. The majority of ads in an established Yellow Pages stay there for more than one year, some of them for years and years and years. They do not stay there if the buyer finds them to be a complete waste of money.

Based on the traffic analysis of Yellow Pages usage discussed in Chapter 4, the above statement is an exaggeration and, like most exaggerations, contains relatively little truth. Perhaps you thought this way when you started to read this book. Hopefully, by now you are not in the same corner as someone who would make or believe this statement.

MYTH #5
YELLOW PAGES ADVERTISING IS HIGHLY OVERRATED

In the majority of cases, the reverse is actually true. The reason the largest ads under a heading work so well is because relatively few businesses buy them. They are effective because of the lack of competition for the user. If more businesses realized the true potential of Yellow Pages, then over time it might become overrated. In some cases, it already has.

There have been and are headings in specific directories that may have reached the stage of being overrated by some advertisers. The headings

ATTORNEYS or LAWYERS in some directories are certainly starting to reach that status. More money is spent in the Yellow Pages by attorneys than any other profession or business. This is a relatively recent phenomenon. The growth of the advertising by this profession has been very rapid. Certainly an attorney who had a full-page ad in a directory ten years ago is not getting the same results from the full-page ad in that directory today. The amount of advertising under the heading ATTORNEYS has grown at such a fast rate that it has almost definitely outgrown the increase in the usage of the heading over that period of time.

A few headings have grown too rapidly over too short a period of time. When this happens, the growth is followed by a decline in the size of the ads or the number of larger ads under the heading in following issues.

The automobile insurance business gets a lot of calls from Yellow Pages advertising. Over a period of years, there was a rapid growth in the number of auto insurance agencies locating in one particular market. Many of the new companies quickly became multiple-location companies in that area. Three things happened as a result of this growth.

First, the number of full-page and three-quarter-page ads grew substantially. Many of the new multiple-location agencies knew the importance of Yellow Pages advertising to their success and bought their ads accordingly.

Second, their entry into the market and their large ads made it increasingly difficult for single-location agencies that had been in the market prior to this growth. The established agencies saw the results from their ads decline because the number of businesses grew faster than the market was growing. Gradually, some of these older one-location agencies started to reduce their Yellow Pages ads, and eventually many of them closed their doors or sold out to other agencies.

Third, because the market became overpopulated with auto insurance agencies, some of the new agencies failed and some of the established multiple-location agencies started to close some of their locations. This resulted in some additional reduction of the larger ads under this heading.

The agencies that are left with the biggest ads are now getting results similar to the results the biggest ads were getting prior to the too rapid growth of competition.

Remember, the reason most businesses never get the results they would like from Yellow Pages advertising is because they fail to be aggressive enough to get those results. That is not the result of overrating Yellow Pages. It is the result of underrating it!

MYTH #6
DO NOT ADVERTISE IN ALL DIRECTORIES THAT SERVE A MARKET, JUST THE BEST ONE

Not all directories are created equal. Some directories get more usage than others. Therefore, some directories deserve more of your financial support than others. This does not mean, however, that a competing directory does not have potential value to you.

Directories only exist because of usage. If they lose usage, they will eventually see a decline in the support from their advertisers. If the usage declines far enough, they will cease to exist.

The most questionable directories are first editions. At that point, they are an idea from which the publisher hopes to make money. Whether or not the advertisers will make money from their ads is usually uncertain. Much depends on who is publishing the directory and the competitive situation in the market it is serving.

Directories that have been published for more than five years have usually developed some degree of established usage. Now the question is how much to spend to take advantage of that usage. Frequently, these directories can be a very good buy—not because they can produce as much business as a directory with greater usage but because it frequently takes relatively few dollars to become an aggressive advertiser in them. Hopefully, by this time, you understand that aggressive Yellow Pages advertising is the effective and profitable way to buy Yellow Pages.

The question is how much additional business you need and want. If you are still in the struggling stages of building a business, you need to examine each directory in your market to determine if it has the potential to generate profitable business for you. If you are trying to find ways to add to an already successful business, you need to do the same thing. The difference is that, percentage-wise, the smaller directories are more important to the struggling, smaller business.

Now let's switch our train of thought from offensive to defensive reasons for advertising. A new, struggling business has less reason to advertise in other directories to keep from losing business. The more established business has to consider the possibility of losing business by not being represented or by having a token presence. New publishers count on established businesses for the base on which to build their product. There is a "gun to the head" aspect to their entrance into a new market. Many advertisers buy in fear that the new directory will be successful.

In the final analysis, the decision should be made according to the amount of usage a given directory appears to have. The number of advertisers, the retention of the advertisers, the growth of the product over a period of years, and the specific market that is served by the directory are the key criteria to use in making your decisions.

MYTH #7
A CLEAN AD IS AN EFFECTIVE AD

This myth was actually dispelled in Chapter 8 on copy. Copy is so important that it is worth reviewing the key points on how to make your ad more productive for you.

Quality of copy is of great importance in an ad. Frequently, you can get a very important message across with relatively few words. Quality copy points are the words that are emphasized in an ad. They appear as headlines, subheadlines, or in other ways of making the words stand out.

The purpose of quantity of copy is to try to appeal to every potential customer using the Yellow Pages that you would like to have as a customer. Chances are you offer a wide variety of products, services, brands, sizes, prices, etc. You do so because your potential customer base is that diverse. If you did not offer all of those things, you would not attract as many customers. Your Yellow Pages ad is no different. You attract users by telling them what you have to offer them. If you leave out important information, you fail to get the calls that information would have generated if it had been in your ad.

Some of the details you can put in an ad are more important than others. If you sell or service brand name products, they belong in your ad by name. If you have unusually convenient operating hours, they belong in your ad. If you cover a large geographical area out of one location and you do business by going to your customer, you need to consider using multiple telephone numbers in your ad.

You want results from your Yellow Pages advertising. The easiest way to increase the results from a "clean" ad is to add important copy that has been missing. Other than increasing the size of your ad, this is the most important change you can make in your Yellow Pages advertising. Follow the logic: More copy hits more people between the eyes. The more people you hit between the eyes, the more responses from your ad.

MYTH #8
ONLY PRICE SHOPPERS USE YELLOW PAGES

This is one of the most common misconceptions about Yellow Pages advertising. Like many opinions concerning Yellow Pages, it is overly simplistic. Of course shoppers use the Yellow Pages. It is a wonderful tool when someone has the time and inclination to look for the best price available. Does that mean every time you or I use the Yellow Pages, all we are looking for is the best price? Of course not. Price is a factor. Sometimes it may be the most important factor. Yet it is not always the most important factor, and in some situations it may be close to meaningless.

There are two reasons for this common misconception. First, since price shoppers do use the Yellow Pages, some of the calls a business will get will be from price shoppers. Yet everyone who asks for a price is not price shopping. Think about your own usage of Yellow Pages. Even if you are not price shopping, don't you usually ask for a price or an estimate of the cost? That's just being a responsible buyer. Yet many business owners put everyone who asks for a price in the category of being a price shopper. What a negative way to look at a potential customer. This type of person thinks all anyone is looking for is the cheapest source for the product or service they are seeking. How do the companies that charge more stay in business if everyone is only buying at the lowest possible cost?

Second, most people who have this opinion are not buyers of relatively large ads under their headings. Since they are not buying relatively large ads for their businesses and practices under their headings, they are not getting a lot of calls from the more selective buyers who are using the Yellow Pages. Their ads do not stand out enough to get a lot of readership, and they do not say enough about their business or practice to attract calls from the more selective Yellow Pages user. This means that a high percentage of the new calls they are getting from Yellow Pages are probably from callers who are doing a lot of price shopping.

It is a self-fulfilling prophesy. Most Yellow Pages advertisers do not believe they can get quality calls from their ads, so they do not buy ads to attract quality calls. Since they do not try to attract these calls, they do not get many of them. What kind of calls do they get for the most part? Price shoppers!

MYTH #9
PEOPLE ARE AFRAID OF FULL-PAGE AND THREE-QUARTER-PAGE ADS BECAUSE THEY LOOK TOO EXPENSIVE

This statement has a lot in common with the previous myth. For the most part, this statement is made by people who have never bought a full-page or three-quarter page ad. Like most opinions, this statement is right some of the time. For example, there are Yellow Pages users who will not call a plumber with a full-page ad because they believe that plumber will charge more than one with a smaller ad. Who do they tell this to? The plumber they call with the smaller ad! Therefore, that plumber draws the conclusion he or she draws.

The statement really does not make sense. If no one is calling the largest ads because they look too expensive, how are the owners of these ads paying for their ads? Obviously they are getting calls, and, in fact, in most cases they are getting a sufficient number of calls to make the large ads profitable for them. Like the advertiser who only gets calls from price shoppers because he or she does not go after the quality calls, the owners of smaller ads do not get many of the calls that the owners of the largest ads under a heading receive.

There are good reasons for the existence of the myths covered in this chapter. They are all partially true. They are all accurate some of the time, but they do not represent the total picture. The key to the total picture is understanding usage and what drives usage. When you advertise in Yellow Pages, you are not just buying an ad. You are buying exposure at a time, for the most part, when someone is ready to purchase something. The results from that advertising are much more dependent upon how and where you represent yourself than on anything the user does. The user is going to do business with somebody. If you give your Yellow Pages advertising the time and consideration it deserves, you will find that the usage has always been there—you just have not been getting your fair share of it. Raise your "comfort level" and raise your results!

MYTH #10
ALL I WILL DO IS SAVE MONEY IF
I CUT MY YELLOW PAGES BUDGET

There is always pressure to control costs. Since I am in business for myself, I know that if I am not good at controlling costs, my business will not be as profitable as it could be. The problem is Yellow Pages is a revenue-producing product for most advertisers. Therefore, you affect your business in two ways when you cut your Yellow Pages budget. There is no doubt one of your expenses on your ledger is reduced. That can be seen very clearly. What can't be seen nearly as well is the effect of the reduction in terms of lost income.

Recall my "mirror" concept as it applies to opinions of advertisers. Most advertisers reflect their negative opinions, so you have a lot of support staring you in the face when you decide to reduce your budget. Recall my comments about some of the Yellow Pages consultants out there. They know you will reduce your Yellow Pages budget if you are convinced you will not be affected negatively by the reduction.

Stop and think about what is more important to you: spending less in Yellow Pages or doing something to increase your income from Yellow Pages. Obviously, most people in business would like to build their business or professional practice to make it larger in the future than it is now. When that is the case, your focus should be more on how to spend additional dollars profitably than on reducing what you are currently spending.

THE YELLOW PAGES SAMPLER

The following pages are intended as a reference for statements made within the text of the book. These pages will help give more meaning to the words as various aspects of Yellow Pages advertising are explained. The pages are based on actual directories to make them as real as possible. The identities of the ads have been changed to protect the innocent. Some of the ads are obviously better than others. The main point is these pages represent reality in terms of number of ads, size of ads, and the content of various ads you will find in directories around the country.

The last four pages of " The Yellow Pages Sampler" are devoted to depicting good and not so good use of Yellow Pages space. These four pages will allow you to see for yourself what happens when an ad that has an incomplete message is revised to improve its sales message. In addition, these pages depict how adding some effective graphics and borders can also change the effectiveness of the message contained within an ad. Finally, you can see for yourself what happens when color is used within an ad, both effectively and relatively ineffectively.

There is one relatively new color process I do not shown in these pages. It is called white knockout. It is not offered by all publishers, but its use is growing rapidly. Instead of a display ad on a yellow background because it is printed on yellow paper, a white knockout ad has a white background. If it is available in a directory you are considering, you will see it. Like all color ads, it is priced at a premium.

None of the ads presented in this section are represented as being perfect. That is because perfection is in the eyes of the beholder. In this book size and content are the two most crucial elements of an ad. The last four pages of this section illustrate ways to improve the visual effectiveness of an ad. In talking with advertisers over the years I have learned there are vast differences in opinion when it comes to the final layout of an ad. If you buy a suitable size ad for your needs and give as complete a picture of your products and services as possible within that space, you will have done your job well. Only you can judge if you are truly satisfied with the overall design. If you are, that is the most important opinion.

I encourage you to examine other Yellow Pages directories and read other texts to learn more about content and design. The more you study other ads, the more you will develop a sense of which are better than others and why you believe them to be better. Copy the better ones and learn what not to do from the others. Remember, the majority of your competitors will never take the time you have taken to make your advertising more effective. Use that knowledge to your advantage.

COMMERCIAL CARPET
OUR SHOWCASE... AT YOUR PLACE

FREE SHOP-AT-HOME MOBILE SHOWROOM SERVICE

LOW MONTHLY PAYMENTS

COMMERCIAL Carpets On The Go
639-3366

SINCE 1968

THE NEWEST DIMENSION IN CUSTOMER SERVICE IN SMITH COUNTY
- Free Consultation By Our Floor Covering Experts
- "Carpet Guard" Applications For Longer Wear And Soil Retardation.
- Exclusive 5 Year Guarantee

2004 Grove Rd. (Across from K-Mart)
FT SMITH

639-3366

DISCOUNTED FLOORING SYSTEMS

**BUY DIRECT FROM MILLS
SAVE UP TO 50%
TOP QUALITY**

HUGE INVENTORY
LARGE SELECTION OF CERAMIC TILE
100'S OF ROOM SIZE REMNANTS
MAJOR BRANDS, DISCOUNTED PRICES

COMPARE-THEM: AS LOW AS	US: AS LOW AS	COMPARE-THEM: AS LOW AS	US: AS LOW AS	COMPARE-THEM: AS LOW AS	US: AS LOW AS
$17.99	$7.99	$21.99	$9.99	$25.99	$11.99

HOURS:
MON-FRI 8-6
SAT 9-5

262-1218

LOCATED:
2024 ORANGE BOULEVARD N.
FT SMITH
(BEHIND PET CENTRAL)

MARKHAM FLOORING

CARPET • VINYL • CERAMIC • WOOD

Professional Installation
Residential • Commercial
AREA RUGS
CAPTURE DRY CARPET CLEANING

26 YEARS EXPERIENCE

ACME PLAZA
4208 ACME RD
FT SMITH

Drive A Little • • • • • • SAVE A LOT

"The Cheap, Cheap Dealer"
762-5380

Building A Reputation YOU Can Stand On
Major Brand Names

I-59 Exit 2 - One Mile East on U.S. 14

Nick's FLOOR COVERINGS

GUARANTEED LOWEST PRICES!!

SEE OUR OFFER IN THE COUPON SECTION

BRAND NAME CARPETS

CARPET
- ALADDIN
- BURLINGTON
- CABIN CRAFT
- CORONET
- EXCLUSIVE
- HORIZON

TILE
- ALADDIN
- IRON ROCK
- KENTILE
- MANNINGTON
- NATURA
- REFFIN

WOOD FLOORING
- ANDERSON
- BRUCE
- DESOTO
- HARTCO
- KAHRS

VINYL
- AMTICO
- ARMSTRONG
- CONGOLEUM
- DOMCO
- KENTILE
- MANNINGTON

1021 RAILROAD AV • LA CROSSE
346-3125

OPEN:
MON-FRI 9AM-6PM
SAT 9AM-5PM SUN BY APPT.

INSTALLATIONS & FINANCING AVAILABLE
Se Habla Español

Oriental Rugs

have enchanted & fascinated people throughout the world

Oldest & Finest Rug Dealer & Cleaner
Serving Smith County for Over 10 Years

Shazam

LARGEST AND FINEST SELECTION OF HAND KNOTTED RUGS IN SMITH COUNTY

HOURS: Monday-Sat. • 9:30 am to 6:00 pm Sunday By Appointment

TOP PRICES PAID FOR OLD RUGS

ORIENTAL RUG GALLERY
Direct Importer of Fine Antique & Contemporary Rugs

364-6060

All work performed by hand with CARE by our native experts

SEE OUR OFFER IN THE COUPON SECTION

Other Showrooms:
Harrisburg
Reading

VISA MasterCard American Express Discover

- **APPRAISALS**
  Certified Appraiser
  Museum Consultant
- **CLEANING**
- **REPAIR**
- **RESTORATION**
- **STORAGE**

SENIOR CITIZENS DISCOUNT

FINANCING AVAILABLE
CHECKS - CASH

Newly Remodeled Showroom
2144 Orange Blvd • La Crosse

CARPET & RUG DEALERS NEW (CONT)

AMERICA'S CARPET PLACE
Carpet - Vinyl - Tile
Thousand of Samples Specializing In:
• Residential & Commercial
• Insurance Replacement
• Color Matching
• Design Assistance

CONTRACTORS	317-0140
FAX	317-4221
6065 SEASIDE RD FT SMITH	317-0005

In Ft Smith Plaza

Andre's Carpet Store
2136 South Rd ------- 867-0140

Artistry In Flooring
Ft Smith ------- 284-9657
La Crosse ------- 333-0007

Authentic Discount Carpets
30811 Central Ave ------- 639-3301

Interior Design Center
344 N.W. 74th St. ------- 245-2263

Bailey's Carpet Center
5071 S. Orange Blvd. Ft. Smith ------- 656-4111

FILLER

BC Interior Design Center, Inc.

Since 1947

YOUR ONE STOP SHOP

245-2263

344 N. W. 74TH STREET

FINANCING AVAILABLE

VISA MasterCard American Express Discover

COMPLETE DESIGN SERVICE

- **QUALITY CARPET**
- **WOOD FLOORING**
- **CERAMIC TILE • VINYL**
- **WALL COVERINGS**
- **MINI/VERTICAL BLINDS**
- **CUSTOM BEDSPREADS**

RESIDENTIAL • COMMERCIAL
LICENSED INTERIOR DESIGNER

Worryfree Congoleum
Stainmaster Scotchgard

"VISIT OUR SHOWROOM"

Y-5

CARPET & RUG DEALERS NEW (CONT)

BEAM FLOOR & DECOR

BEAM FLOOR & DECOR
"Since 1966"

**CARPETING
CERAMIC TILE
VERTICALS
FLOORING**
$5,0000 INSTANT CREDIT
No Money Down to Qualified Buyers
In Home Shopping
FREE ESTIMATES
Notice Our New Location
10191 Orange Blossom Boulevard
Ft Smith

"We Create Beautiful Lifestyles"

10191 Orange Blossom Boulevard -364-0002
4022 Goldenrod Ave La Crosse ----593-5252

Bensen's Carpet Showroom
11991 N. Grover Rd --------------------637-6717
BEST MOBILE CARPET SALES & SERVICE
SEE AD IN LA CROSSE BOOK
--963-3133
Bon Ton Carpets
14934 N Orange Ave----------------------714-0044
Borden's Carpet Outlet
10541 N. U.S. 14--------------------------814-0521
Cain Carpet
2271 Magnolia Avenue---------------------854-8291
CAROL'S CUSTOM FLOOR COVERING
SHOP AT HOME SERVICE
--284-0645
Carpet Central USA
2254 Santiago Ave------------------------245-3468
Carpet Store The
9411 S. Central Blvd----------------------799-0007
CARPET WHOLESALE
1005 N. Grove Ave. Ft Smith---------639-0037

CHEMICAL CLEANING SERVICE

CHEMICAL CLEANING SERVICE

Carpet • Upholstery • Draperies
Featuring:
A Natural Carpet Cleaning Process
You and Your Family Will Love
No Steam • No Shampoo
No Dry Powder

945-1991

Independently Owned & Operated
Serving Ft. Smith County
(Except La Crosse)

3104 NW 7th St -------------------------945-1991

Color Carpet Center
45311 Grover Rd -----------------------639-6366
COMMERCIAL CARPETS ON THE GO
2004 Grove Rd ------------------------639-3366
Carter Pat Carpet Central USA
2254 Santiago Ave. --------------------245-3468

FILLER

Harrison
THE CARPET SPECIALIST

43 Years Of Service In Smith County

Carpet • Area Rugs • Draperies
Ceramic Tile • Vinyl • Wood Flooring

Lifetime Guarantee On Materials & Labor

Come Visit Our Showrooms:

15521 Grover Rd	8871 James Rd	4143 Dean Rd
638-0096	**433-7351**	**945-4417**
FT SMITH	FT SMITH	LA CROSSE

VISA MasterCard

ALSO IN HARRISBURG, READING AND BLOOMSBURG

Every Day Low Prices

Professional Personalized Service for Over 34 Years

All Major Brands Available
* **Carpet**
* **Ceramic Tile**
* **Wood**
* **Vinyl**

Open 7 Days

DAY-DATED CARPET

Featuring Wear-Dated Carpet By Monsanto
Full 5 Year & Stain Warranties
The Latest In Colors & Styles

284-0067

3461 N. Orange Blvd.
(5 Miles North Of University)

VISA MasterCard

Financing Available

WJC
Wayne Jones Carpet

A & H Carpet Center

"SERVING FT. SMITH COUNTY SINCE 1977"

CARPET • VINYL
CERAMIC TILE • WOOD

- All Material & Workmanship Guaranteed
- Professional Installation
- Free Estimates

939-7487
1064 FOREST AV.
(Colonial & Forest Intersection)

VISA / MasterCard

Designer's RUG BOUTIQUE

434-4859
759 82nd St. S.
Just off Central Blvd.
Opposite Ft. Smith Mall

- Wholesale To Designers
- Direct Importers And Distributors Of Hand Knotted Oriental Rugs
- Wide Selection Of Contemporary, Custom And Decorative Rugs, Tapestries, Kelims, And Runners

FOR ALL YOUR AREA RUG NEEDS

FREE DELIVERY IN FT. SMITH

Elegant Flooring

Sales and Installation
Formal and Mobile Showroom
Decorator Service

A Complete Selection Of Floors & Walls

- Ceramic
- Marble
- Granite
- Glass Block
- Wallpaper
- Carpet
- Vinyl
- Wood
- Cultured Marble
- Custom Area Rugs

Ft. Smith Mall
10361 S. Central Blvd.
Ft. Smith (Next To Frank's Steaks)

- Commercial
- Residential

Phone 814-3548
Fax 814-9555

FLOOR COVERINGS

CARPET • VINYL • PARQUET • CERAMIC TILE

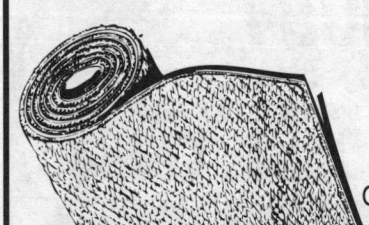

PAUL'S RUG SHOWCASE

6365 Old Forge Av.
984-2032

CARPET & RUG DEALERS NEW (CONT)

CREATIVE CARPETS & TILE
SERVING LA CROSSE FOR OVER 16 YEARS
• CARPET • TILE
• VINYL • WOOD
We Specialize In Personal Service
RESIDENTIAL & COMMERCIAL
FREE ESTIMATES
2978 COMMERCIAL BLVD LA CROSSE----- 594-5311

Culpepper Carpet & Vinyl
5211 Homewood Ave S.----------863-B611
CUSTOM FLOORING OF FT. SMITH
16801 HOLSTEIN AVE----------396-8000
Davis Decorating Center
1274 Indiana Road----------549-3131
Designer's Rug Boutique
759 82nd St S.   434-4855
(See Our Display Ad On This Page)
DESIGNERS SHOWROOM OF LA CROSSE
7074 NW 6TH AVE----------245-4662
Discounted Floor Systems
2024 Orange Blvd Ft Smith----------262-1218
(See Our Display Ad On Page 2)
Discount Carpet Wholesalers
9938 Big Rock Ave----------599-8555
DONE RIGHT CARPETS
424 NW 74TH AVE----------405-0700
Donnelley Floor Covering
10067 Millionaire Rd----------762-3377
DUPONT APPROVED MASTERSTORES
MASTERSTORE RETAILERS
Colorful Carpets & Tile
800 Tradewinds Ave----------886-1608
Wayne Jones Carpet
3461 N. Orange Blvd----------284-2867
DUTCHMAN CARPET SHOWCASE
----------277-7574
Elegant Flooring
10361 S. Central Blvd----------814-3548

FAMOUS FLOOR COVERINGS
RESIDENTIAL & COMMERCIAL
Carpets
• Queen • Mohawk
• Inteloom • Aladdin
Wood Flooring
• Anderson • Bruce
• Hartco
Vinyl Flooring
• Armstrong
Ceramic Tile
"We Install What We Sell"
762-0042
29171 Allentown Rd.
Ft. Smith

Flooring Professionals Inc.
8191 NW Santiago Rd----------854-2225
FT SMITH FLOOR COVERINGS
Serving Ft Smith County Since 1983
• CARPET • TILE
• VINYL • WOOD
• CUSTOM WINDOW TREATMENT
Visit Our Showroom or Let Us
Bring Our Showroom To You
2978 COMMERCIAL BLVD LA CROSSE----- 594-5311

GALLAGHER & ASSOCIATES INTERIOR DESIGNERS
BIG TREE SQUARE----------639-1321

FILLER

CARPET & RUG DEALERS NEW (CONT)

GEORGE'S CARPET DEPOT

GCD

"Beautiful Carpets At A Price You Can Afford"

- BEAUTIFUL CARPET DIRECT FROM THE MILLS OF DALTON, LA GRANDGE, WEST POINT, AND OTHER FAMOUS MAKES
- HUGE DISCOUNTS NEVER BEFORE AVAILABLE IN FT. SMITH

MILL DIRECT PRICES ON OVER 500 ROLLS

MONDAY-SATURDAY: 9 AM-7 PM
SUNDAY 1 PM-5 PM

5034 INDEPENDENCE RD -------- 872-2255

HARRISON THE CARPET SPECIALIST
8871 JAMES RD -------- 433-7351
(See Our Display Ad On Page 5)
HOLIDAY CARPETS & FLOORS OF DISTINCTION
15732 N. GROVER RD -------- 939-9122
INDEPENDENCE CARPET STORE
202 HOMEWOOD AVE -------- 963-5333
202 HOMEWOOD AVE -------- 963-4645
Jackson Carpets
8231 Purdue St -------- 945-4040
Kelly's Carpet
108 Magnolia Av -------- 324-2103
LEADING CARPET RETAILERS
5547 AGELESS BLVD -------- 334-2662
Leonard's & Sue's La Crosse Home
Decorating -------- 963-3856
MADISON'S CARPETS
6603 DATE ST -------- 233-2150

FLOORING Professionals, Inc.

CARPET • CERAMIC TILE • VINYL
AREA RUGS • WALLPAPER • WINDOW COVERINGS

SHOP WHERE THE BUILDERS GO FOR NEW HOME DISCOUNTS

FREE ESTIMATE 854-2225

LOWEST PRICES LARGEST SELECTION

8191 NW Santiago Rd (Across from Goodyear)

VISA MasterCard

QUALITY FLOORING & TILE

Carpet • Vinyl • Tile • Area Rugs • Wood • Vertical/Blinds

Call THE SHOP AT HOME EXPERTS

FREE MEASUREMENT • FREE QUOTES

CALL For Our Price Before You Buy

245-0072

6331 La Crosse Rd

- Custom Installation
- Serving Ft. Smith County For Over 20 Years

VISA MasterCard

Mark's Floor Coverings
42188 Alston Rd -------- 762-3G30
MOHAWK CARPET
A & H Flooring
1064 Forest Ave -------- 939-7497
Newton Floor Systems
13941 Big River Dr -------- 334-6161
Nick's Floor Coverings
1021 Railroad Ave La Crosse -------- 346-9125
(See Our Display Ad On Page 3)
Paul's Rug Showcase
6365 Old Forge Ln -------- 565-7676
(See Our Display Ad On Page 6)
Quality Flooring & Tile
6331 La Crosse Rd -------- 245-0072
(See Our Display Ad On This Page)
Quality Flooring & Tile
6331 La Crosse Rd -------- 245-0072
Rags To Riches Rugs
3071 Oak Forest Ln -------- 664-0013
Schoolhouse Rugs
504 Highlands Rd -------- 478-7665

SHAZAM ORIENTAL RUGS & GALLERY
-------- 364-6060
(See Our Display Ad On Page 4)
SMITH'S INSTALLATIONS
7412 ANDREWS RD -------- 334-5112

SUNSHINE FLOORING & DECOR CENTER

SUNRISE FLOOR COVERING & INTERIORS
• CARPET • TILE
• VINYL • VERTICALS
CUSTOM DRAPERIES

ALL YOUR FLOOR COVERING NEEDS

854-0101

88 VENICE DR LA CROSSE -------- 854-0101

Super Prices in Rugs
107237 Island Hwy. -------- 762-0133
TRUMAN'S CARPET CENTER
4053 LA CROSSE RD -------- 433-6568

Value & Discount Carpet Warehouse Center
9571 Ohio Blvd -------- 572-7096
WALL & FLOOR WORLD
4811 OHIO BLVD -------- 638-4717
WAYNE JONES CARPET
General Offices
1587 Warehouse Rd -------- 762-0067
WAYNE JONES CARPET SHOWROOM
1643 N. ORANGE BLVD -------- 284-0067
1587 WAREHOUSE RD -------- 762-0067
(See Our Display Ad On Page 5)
YOUNG'S CARPET SALES
1484 EASY STREET RD -------- 364-4143

CARPET & RUG DEALERS USED

Brooks Furniture & Antiques
8621 Calloway Rd -------- 284-0036
MAJOR FINE ARTS BUYERS
4331 SEASHELL AVE -------- 594-9667

CARPET & RUG DYERS

A Sure Bet Dyeing & Cleaning Co
116 NW 44th St -------- 277-4414
AMERICA'S BEST CARPET CLEANING SERVICE
FT SMITH -------- 639-4333

CARPET COLOR SPECIALISTS

CCS Carpet Color Specialists

345-3555

SMITH COUNTY SINCE 1973
WE MEET OR BEAT ALL AREA DYE PRICES & GUARANTEES

DYE SPECIAL
Bring back to life!
Stained & faded carpets

ANY COLOR

AS LOW AS $69.95

PREVENT FADING

FREE COLOR "As Low As $49.95"
Furnished LR DA HALL
with every carpet cleaned

-------- 345-35555

Power Carpet Cleaning -------- 963-0001
Professional Carpet Care
La Crosse -------- 475-5154
Tru-Clean Service -------- 664-866

CARPET & RUG LAYERS

ADVANCED FLOORING INSTALLATION

★ DIAL DIRECT ★
With Installer, **Save $**
• All Type Of Carpet
• Vinyl, Tile & Wood
  & Specialty Rubber & Inlaid
• Sub Flooring, Install & Repair
• Honest, Professional - 13 Yrs. Exp.
License # 55114

-------- 762-6082

FILLER

BALDWIN'S FLOORING

Serving Smith County For Over 14 Yrs.
RESIDENTIAL & COMMERCIAL
Tile-Carpet-Vinyl
SERVICE - INSTALLATION
Free Estimates - Financing Available

5582 LABOR RD -------- 733-4434

CAROL'S CUSTOM FLOOR COVERING
-------- 284-0645
Harvey's Flooring
9711 Miami Blvd -------- 475-7163
Smith's Installations
7412 Andrews Rd -------- 334-5112

CARPET & RUG REPAIRING

ACTIVE CARPET CARE

CARPET REPAIRS
• Restretch • Broken Seams Repaired
• Tinting • Dyeing
• Spot Dyeing • Burns • Holes
**CARPET SALES
INSTALLATION
STEAM/DRY CLEANING**
• Upholstery • Carpet • Drapes
• Pet Odor Removal
• 24 Hour Flood Damage
Licensed & Insured
277-1011
-------- 664-0900

Baron John S.
1957 Alabama Bay Rd -------- 615-0141
BOWEN'S CARPET SERVICES
5951 IRISH ST -------- 664-0626
Cummings Floor Repair -------- 639-6562

SHAZAM ORIENTAL RUGS & GALLERY
OLDEST & FINEST
RUG DEALER & CLEANING
Repair & Restoration
By Hand With Care By
Our Native Experts
• Water & Flood Damage
• Smoke Damage
• Spot & Stain Removal
• Color Restoration
Hours: Mon-Sat 9:30 am-6:00 pm
Sunday By Appointment
(Please See Our Offer In The Coupon Section)

2144 FT. SMITH BLVD -------- 364-6060

STANLEY'S CARPET CARE
Home Of The
Carpet Surgeons
• The Repair Specialists •
• Burns • Holes • Tinting
• Broken Seams • Redesigns
• Stain Removal • Re-Stretching
Complete Carpet Cleaning
• Furniture • Drapes • Verticals
• Pet Odor • Dupont Teflon
24 HOUR EMERGENCY SERVICE
Carpet Sales & Installation
Free Offer In Coupon Section
-------- 540-1059

TOM'S FLOORS
We Repair All Types Of
Carpet & Linoleum
Burns • Permanent Spots
Seams • Wrinkles
24 Hour Emergency Service
Free Estimates
1697 MAGNOLIA LN -------- 284-6324

FILLER

Y-8

CARPET WORKROOMS

John's Carpets ----------------------------------- 382-8894

CARPORTS

ADVANTAGE MOBILE HOME SYSTEMS
1332 SW MAPLE ST ----------------------- 345-5151
FRANK'S ALUMINUM SERVICE CO.
4162 INDIANA AVE ------------------------ 233-7633

Graham Ron Aluminum & Vinyl ---------------------------- 277-4799
Inside Remodelers
4391 Andrews St ---------------------------------- 872-7363

FILLER

BILLINGS RETAIL DATA SYSTEMS
RETAIL DATA SYSTEMS
SALES • SERVICE • RENTALS
24 HR LOCAL SERVICE
RESTAURANT SYSTEMS
P.O.S. COMPUTER SYSTEMS
SERVICE CONTRACTS
726-7212
LA CROSSE ---------------------------- 726-7212

Cash Register Medic
5461 San Pedro Dr ------------------- 454-0005
(See Our Display Ad On This Page)

CASH REGISTER MEDIC
A Division Of
Business Services & Systems
Featuring: **ESPER & SAMSUNG** CASH REGISTERS
FREE ESTIMATES
SALES • SERVICE • LEASING
FOR MOST MAJOR BRANDS
454-0005
RING IN NEW *Values*
Panasonic 5461 SAN PEDRO DR
FT SMITH

DAVID'S CASH REGISTER COMPUTER SERVICE
• SALES
• SERVICE
• SUPPLIES
• PROGRAMMING

ALL MAJOR BRANDS
Most Reasonable
Prices Around

24 HOUR SERVICE

549-3913

5035 Oceanview Dr
La Crosse

5035 OCEANVIEW DR ----------------- 549-3913

PREMIER Hospitality Service

"Tomorrow's Technology, For Today's Profit"
TOUCH SCREEN SYSTEMS FOR:
• POINT-OF-SALE   • INVENTORY
• LABOR MANAGEMENT • FREQUENT DINING
• ACCOUNTING   • SERVER & PATRON PAGING
• REPORTING   • 24 HOUR SERVICE

- STATE WIDE -
1-800-177-0017
FT. SMITH 772-7710

LEONARD'S ALUMINUM COMPANY
QUALITY WORKMANSHIP
FREE ESTIMATES
273240CBC
8372 KANT RD ---------------------- 233-9995

MASTER'S QUALITY SHEDS
5075 FOREST AVE ------------------ 939-2214
PROFESSIONAL ALUMINUM CO.
6075 OLDHAM BLVD ---------------- 814-0552
Specialized Aluminum & Carpentry
1561 Central Blvd --------------------- 867-3223
TURNER HOME SERVICES CORP.
LA CROSSE ----------------------- 963-5903

CASH REGISTERS & SUPPLIES

A B D EQUIPMENT CO.
DIGITAL DINING
TEC
MAIRED
SWEDA
Local People • Local Service
KRONOS TIME CLOCKS
Supplies For All Makes
615-6162
The Complete System Solution
5512 CITY BLVD. ------------------ 615-6162

A B D Equipment Co.
5512 City Blvd. ---------------------- 615-6162
(See Our Display Ad On This Page)

BEST BUSINESS SYSTEMS OF LA CROSSE
• Cash Registers
• POS/Computers
• Bar Code Readers &
  Inventory Controls
• Fax and Scales
SALES • SERVICE • SUPPLIES
-------------------------------- 665-9995

HARVARD DATA SYSTEMS
------------------------- 1-800-417-2441
Innovative Electronics & Systems Inc.
------------------------- 1-800-324-6404
(See Our Display Ad On This Page)
Premier Hospitality Service
5311 Colonial Rd -------------------- 772-7701
(See Our Display Ad On This Page)

TEC ELECTRONIC CASH REGISTERS
A Complete Line
Of Electronic
Cash Register
Systems Customized
For Your Business   **TEC**

"FOR SALES & INFORMATION CALL"
AUTHORIZED DEALER
Reading Cash Register Co.
729 ORANGE AVE READING -------- 1-800-923-8854

CASTERS & GLIDES

THE GAMING PLACE
605 3RD AVE BLOOMSBURG --------- 896-3131

CARTER EQUIPMENT CO.
CASTERS/WHEELS
• Industrial • Institutional
• Furniture
ALL MANUFACTURERS
★★★★ In Stock ★★★★
TOLL FREE-DIAL"1" & THEN
-------------------------- 800-888-1794

DECO TRUCKS-CASTERS & WHEELS
AUTHORIZED DEALER
Davis Equipment
4217 SE 27th St Paoli
Toll Free Dial "1" & Then ----------- 800-154-0300

ABD Equipment Co.   micros
COMPUTERIZED SYSTEMS

TOUCH SCREEN/KEYBOARD SYSTEMS

LOCAL PEOPLE
LOCAL SERVICE   **615-6162**   SUPPLIES FOR
ALL MAKES
5512 City Blvd.   FT. SMITH

NCR An AT&T Company **iES** Innovative Electronics & Systems, Inc.

"AUTHORIZED DISTRIBUTORS"

HOSPITALITY SYSTEMS   SCANNING SYSTEMS
• Touch Screens   800-324-6404   • Frequent Shopper
• Inventory   • FM Terminals
• Frequent Dining   • Label Printing

"SOLVING OUR CUSTOMERS' PROBLEMS TODAY"

FILLER

FILLER

CATALOG SHOWROOMS

Lawson's
 5064 Ohio Blvd --------------------------------- 639-0006

CATERERS

A Fine Affair
 5461 San Pedro Dr ------------------------------ 664-5221
ANDERSON'S RIB JOINT
 See Our Ad at Restaurants
 2561 INDIAN BLVD ------------------------------ 284-8007
ATWOOD'S FAMILY BUFFET
 1907 UNIVERSITY DR --------------------------- 939-7773
Big Bear Catering
 6151 NW 2nd St --------------------------------- 475-7287
BLOWING ROCK GOLF & TENNIS COUNTRY CLUB FT SMITH
 500 BLOWING ROCK DR. ------------------------ 233-4337
Cakes To Go
 9432 Forest Ave -------------------------------- 639-0402
Caldwell's Catering
 4589 Cabbage St La Crosse --------------------- 984-0822
CAPTAIN'S CAFE THE
 109 ADMIRAL DR -------------------------------- 945-1004
Carson City Volunteer Fireman's Assoc Inc
 3131 NW 74th St -------------------------------- 549-2208
CAROL'S CATERING SERVICE
 3271 GOLDENROD RD --------------------------- 274-4762
Carter's Catering
 4234 SE 72nd St -------------------------------- 382-6891
Cater Queen
 8092 Trucking Rd ------------------------------- 433-4408
Cater Queen NE Inc.
 8023 Trucking Rd ------------------------------- 433-4408
Catering At Its Finest
 2421 Oilwell Blvd ------------------------------- 867-7272
Catering By Louise
 2431 Center St --------------------------------- 475-6602
Catering International
 1418 University Dr ----------------------------- 984-2262
Chef Tom's Catering
 2212 First Ave Ft Smith ------------------------ 733-3811
Club Exotique
 261 Rip Van Winkle St ------------------------- 939-6060
Cooper's Cafe & Catering
 578 Magnolia Ln -------------------------------- 284-8882
Customized Catering & Parties
 Big Rock Sq ------------------------------------- 334-8315
DANNY'S OPEN PIT BAR-B-QUE
 Not Just Barbeque
 Closed Mondays
 15711 Hwy 8 ----------------------------------- 496-5993
Delong's Catering
 2020 Santa Ana Dr ----------------------------- 475-7575
 (See Our Display Ad On Page 10)
Dining In Splendor
 --- 454-0090
DUNES COUNTRY CLUB
 949 PALACE DR --------------------------------- 274-5533
FAT AL'S BAR-B-Q
 1461 N. MAIN ST -------------------------------- 799-2897
GABRIEL'S ITALIAN RESTAURANT
 9721 KENMORE DR. ----------------------------- 572-6700
GOLDEN ORIENT CHINESE AMERICAN RESTAURANT
 1071 SAN PEDRO DR --------------------------- 664-7707
Grandpa's
 1719 University Dr ----------------------------- 814-0060
Grandpa's
 5204 Forest Dr --------------------------------- 639-3828
Grandpa's
 563 Reading Ave ------------------------------- 496-7200
I GOT GREAT FOOD
 3721 KENMORE RD FT SMITH ------------------ 639-0990
IGUANA MEXICAN RESTAURANT
 7201 LA CROSSE BLVD ------------------------- 549-5577
KITCHEN WIZARD THE
 5144 MAIN ST ----------------------------------- 572-4345
Klassic Kreations
 1121 NW 43rd St -------------------------------- 245-4633
LOMBARDI'S ITALIAN RESTAURANT & DELI
 1431 NW 74TH ST ------------------------------- 245-1501
MAGICAL WOK
 9006 CROSSROADS SQ ------------------------- 615-6602
Main Event Catering
 --- 814-7535
MANNING'S CAFE & GRILL
 3741 GOLDENROD RD -------------------------- 274-0075
 (See Our Display Ad On This Page)

We Cater To You!

**Weddings • Receptions • Breakfasts
Box Lunches • Cocktail Parties
Banquets • Luncheons • Party Platters**

WE CATER TO YOUR BUSINESS AND PERSONAL NEEDS - AT YOUR PLACE OR OURS

The Official Caterer to the City of
Ft. Smith Convention Center & Arena

Chef Tom's Catering

733-3811

2212 First Av.

Rolling Along Bar-B-Q & Catering Inc

NOBODY DOES IT BETTER!

Monthly Specials
Prime Rib • Surf & Turf • Etc
"Call For Quotes"
"Grilling Hot Dogs To Whole Hogs"

• FUND RAISERS
• CORPORATE PARTIES
• OPEN HOUSES
• GOLF OUTINGS, ETC.

Award Winning Bar-B-Q & Catering

• Featuring •
World Class Ribs
Chicken, Beef,
Pork & Seafood

Quality Catering Since 1978

TOLL FREE FROM FT. SMITH & LA CROSSE
299-9686
LIC. # G4 22082R-2

MANNING'S CAFE & GRILL

Full Service Catering

FRESH SEAFOOD

Your Party Customized Personally By Our Experienced Professional Staff
No Affair Too Large Or Too Small

All Occasions

274-0075

3741 Goldenrod Rd • Bloomsburg

Y-10

Cooper's Cafe & Catering

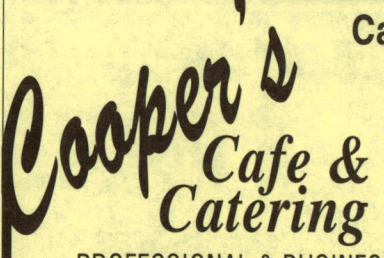

Catering Menus Available Upon Request

284-8882

• PROFESSIONAL & BUSINESS FUNCTIONS • SOCIAL EVENTS
Everything From Hors d'oeuvres To Complete Dinners

VISA MasterCard

578 Magnolia Ln

Delong's CATERING
Since 1954

Delicious Catering At Delectable Prices   **FULL Service Caterers**
Complete Dinners • Beef, Italian Dishes, Poultry, Complete Deli Catering

"WE DO IT ALL" • ALL TYPES OF PARTIES Outdoor • Indoor • Office • Or Hall

WEDDINGS OUR SPECIALTY   **475-7575**
Ask For Claude For Free Estimates   2020 Santa Ana Dr.

PARTY TIME CATERING

Personalized Service with a Reasonable Price

"Choose Your Caterer As Carefully As You Choose Your Guests..."

COMPLETE SERVICES: SET-UP TO CLEAN-UP
• Weddings • Banquets
• Private Parties
• Picnics • Club Functions
• Concessions • Buffets

277-8853
FREE CONSULTATION

BIG BEAR CATERING

Tailor Made Menu's
Beautiful Presentation
Excellent Service

Your Wedding Specialists

Banquets
Sit Down Dinners   **475-7287**   Business Meetings
Parties All Sizes

6151 NW 2nd St • La Crosse

CARTER'S Catering

AFFAIRS OF ANY KIND ANYWHERE ANYTIME

382-6891

A Division of
Big Time Promotions

CATERERS (CONT)

MARS CATERING

CATERING FOR ALL OCCASIONS
• Weddings • Parties
• Corporate Affairs
FRESH, HOMEMADE FOOD

6040 CALLOWAY LN —————————— 939-8411

McDonald's Grille
  3853 McDonald Rd Ft Smith ———— 939-0037
MERCHANT'S RESTAURANT & BAR
  See Our Ad At Restaurants
  9031 HWY 40 ———————————— 396-3222
METROPOLITAN DELI
  5121 MAIN ST ———————————— 867-4533
Mickey's Wonderful Bagel & Deli
  5011 N. Ohio Blvd ———————— 639-1183
MINNELLI'S ITALIAN CAFE
  Specialty Pastas
  ————————————————————— 984-9992
Moon River Continental Restaurant Deli & Lounge
  1907 University Av. ——————— 938-4435
Murphy's Feast
  744 San Pedro Ave ——————— 364-9797
  (See Our Display Ad On Page 11)

NATURE'S FINEST CATERING

"Full Service Catering"
Formal or Informal
We Make Your Party Special,
With All The Personal Touches,
From Planning To The Finale!
FLOWERS, CAKES, DECORATIONS
"We Work Within Your Budget"
MEMBER ASSOCIATION OF BRIDAL CONSULTANTS

2272 SKYVIEW ST ——————— 854-6441
——————————————————— 854-2025

Nature's Finest Catering
  La Crosse ——————————— 854-2025
Nature's Finest Catering
  2272 Skyview St ———————— 854-6441
Party Time Catering
  ——————————————————— 277-8853
  (See Our Display Ad On This Page)
Polly's Famous Chicken Ribs & Burgers
  8323 Forest Ave ———————— 572-2224
Randy's Custom Catering
  1721 Calloway Ln ——————— 984-4244
  (See Our Display Ad On Page 11)

FILLER

Y-11

CATERERS (CONT)

RIBS & MORE BAR-B-Q

BAR-B-Q
"On Site Cooking Available"
Voted Best Bar-B-Q
5 Consecutive Years
• Ribs • Chicken • Steaks
–We Go Anywhere–
945-7247
"Ribs & More's Baby Back Ribs Are Quite Simply The Best We've Ever Had!"
John Lawson, Ft. Smith Daily Reader

Ft. Smith - La Crosse
- Reading & Paoli-
6384 BERNSTEIN AVE ----------- 945-7247

Rolling Along Bar-B-Q & Catering
6993 Ft. Smith Crossing Rd Ft. Smith Crossing -298-9686
(See Our Display Ad On Page 9)
SANTA'S HOUSE RESORT & SPA
6271 CHRISTMAS LN ----------- 664-0004
SCHULTZ'S DELI
9921 N. OHIO BLVD ----------- 572-0213
Singapore Chinese Restaurant & Lounge
1254 Santiago Ave ----------- 945-9995

SHERIDAN PLACE HOTEL

S

We Do It All! The Ideal Setting And Location For Banquets, Business Meetings, Conventions, Rehearsal Dinners, & Private Parties
We Are The WEDDING SPECIALISTS Of South Florida.
• Over 10,000 Sq. Ft. Banquet Rooms
• Personalized & Professional Services
• The Finest In Menu Selection
• Elegant Dining - Excellent Food
• Free Parking - Convenient Location

"We Are Here To Serve You"
733-0030
205 Thomas Dr • Downtown Ft Smith

FILLER

Catering By Louise

475-6602
24 HOUR ANSWERING

"Famous for serving the freshest foods and providing the finest service in Smith County"

For All Events, Personal, Business and Organizations

Office **639-3330**
Fully Insured
License No. 2-R55320-64

Randy's CUSTOM CATERING

Catering With A Personal Touch

Serving Smith County Since 1978

984-4244

Specializing in:
• Weddings
• Professional Staff
• Corporate or Social
• Full Bar Service

1721 Calloway Ln • Ft Smith

TROPHY CUSTOM CATERING

• Complimentary in House Design Service • 
• Parties Of All Sorts!
• Galas
• Buffets - Visually Impressive -

24 HR ANSWERING 733-9678
572-2735
DIGITAL PAGER 633-1055
Lic. & Ins. 20 Yrs. Experience

Murphy's Feast CATERERS

ON & OFF PREMISE
664-3663
364-9797
FAX 364-6471
LIC # 2R397306-4

FILLER

SONNY'S FINE CATERING
Call Mon-Fri 9 AM-5 PM
8095 RIP VAN WINKLE DR ----------- 814-5511
Tootsie's Picnics
3853 Calloway Dr ----------- 939-0037
Trophy Custom Catering
9081 Mark Road ----------- 572-2735
(See Our Display Ad On This Page)
WALT'S DELI
5512 SPENCER ST NW ----------- 814-7092
WONG'S RIB JOINT
8573 OHIO AVE ----------- 939-0013
WOOD'S BARBECUE
10131 S. OHIO AVE ----------- 997-4241

CAULKING CONTRACTORS

ACE PAINTING & CONTRACTING INC.
2944 WHOLESALE DR READING ----------- 346-5267
J&J Masonry & Caulking
Ft Smith ----------- 234-6060
Fax Line ----------- 234-9090
Top Notch Painting & Waterproofing Inc.
Ft Smith ----------- 733-2100

CAULKING MATERIALS & EQUIPMENT

Construction Materials Inc.
402 Main St ----------- 572-5664

CEILINGS CLEANING

ACE CEILING SYSTEMS
----------- 594-1001
CEILING PROS OF FT SMITH COUNTY
----------- 572-3387

CEILINGS CONTRACTORS

ACOUSTIC CEILINGS CORP.
Slate License # GCC 197020
2063 LABOR DR ----------- 233-0161
ALL DRYWALL & CEILING REPAIRS
----------- 475-2081
Ceilings By Tom
----------- 345-4656
Closets by Bea
1172 Winter Dr ----------- 572-1556
Davis & Brown Insulation & Acoustics Inc.
Branch Ofc
721 Retail Blvd La Crosse ----------- 233-8895
DENTON'S CEILINGS
5802 SPENCER DR ----------- 284-3155
DOMED CEILINGS
7302 ABC Blvd La Crosse ----------- 733-4242
Domes of Distinction
----------- 533-4289
DOME CEILINGS IN A DAY
----------- 475-6698
DRYWALL REPAIR SPECIALISTS
----------- 475-9186

KITCHEN HI•LIGHTS

SALES SERVICE REPAIRS

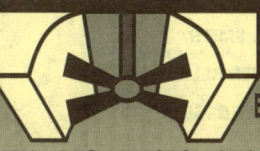

OVER 14 YRS. EXPERIENCE

BEST QUALITY • BEST PRICES • CUSTOM BUILT
Replacement Of Old Yellow Panels Makes Your Kitchen Look Like New

533-4289
ONE DAY INSTALLATION

Y-12

Robert Mason, M. D.

Adult Adolescent & Geriatric Psychiatry Specializing In Cognitive Behavior Psychotherapy & Psychopharmaco Therapy Psychiatry

- Panic Disorder
- Anxiety • Depression
- Stress Management
- Post Traumatic Stress
- Marital Problems & Divorce
- Other Emotional & Behavior Disorders

Diplomate American Society of Psychology & Neurology

477-1006

MOST INSURANCE PLANS ACCEPTED/PAYMENT PLUS AVAILABLE

OFFICE APPOINTMENTS ONLY FLEXIBLE HOURS

PHYSICIANS & SURGEONS-M.D.- PULMONARY DISEASES (LUNGS) Cont.

Spinelli Allen D. Md
7402 Saxony Ave Ft Smith -------- 987-2818

PHYSICIANS & SURGEONS-M.D.- RADIOLOGY

PHYSICIANS & SURGEONS- M.D.-PSYCHIATRY

MORRISON RONALD MD
Child • Adolescent • Adult
Panic • Anxiety • Depression & Other Mood Disorders
- Personality Disorders
- Assertiveness & Co-Dependency Issues
- Drug & Alcohol Rehabilitation
Convenient Location
Medicare Assignment Accepted
If No Answer ----------- 1-800-547-4646
300 N. Main St Ft. Smith ---------- 577-2200

OLDS SAMUEL T MD
143 UNIVERSITY PARKWAY JVLLE----------- 852-5546

PHYSICIANS & SURGEONS-M.D.- PULMONARY DISEASES (LUNGS) Cont.

FT SMITH PULMONARY GROUP PULMONARY ASSOCIATES
BREATHING DISORDERS
ASTHMA • EMPHYSEMA • BRONCHITIS
Gregory A. Eason, M.D., Larry Gilbert, M.D.
William Sands, M.D.
Medical Plaza
1052 N. Lemon Dr Ft Smith ----------- 698-0495

SPINELLI ALLEN D MD
Diplomate American Brd. of Internal Medicine
Diplomate American Brd. of Pulmonary Med.
Medicare Assignment Accepted
709 S Rock St Ft Smith ------------ 228-1804
7402 Saxony Ave Ft Smith ----------- 987-2818

CENTER CITY RADIATION THERAPY ASSOCIATES
806 PEACH TREE DR --------------- 228-2055
Downtown Radiology Inc.
607 E Lake Jane St Ft Smith --------- 333-6679
Downtown Radiology Inc.
5551 Saxony Ave Ft Smith ---------- 475-6886
LITTON ADAMS AND DAVIS MD
1565 SAXONY AVE FT SMITH --------- 235-4900
MAMMOGRAPHY CLINIC ----------- 235-5900
ULTRASOUND CENTER ------------- 235-6900
Morris Hayes Howard Carson & Mason
507 E Dodge St Ft Smith ------------ 837-8840
PETERSON MICHAEL A MD
806 PEACH TREE DR --------------- 228-2055
County Medical Center
Breast Center Ft Smith -------------- 518-8115
(See Our Display Ad On This Page)

FILLER

PHYSICIANS & SURGEONS-M.D.- PSYCHIATRY-CHILD

MARSHALL JOHN H MD
101 TIMBERLINE BLVD LA CROSSE----------- 303-8185
Olds Samuel T MD
La Crosse------------- 228-9296

PHYSICIANS & SURGEONS-M.D.- PULMONARY DISEASES (LUNGS)

FULLER PULMONARY CONSULTANTS PA
FPC
- BREATHING DISORDERS
- LUNG DISEASES

Frank Ferris, M.D.
Donald S. Stevens, M.D.
MEDICARE & MOST INSURANCE ACCEPTED AND FILED
CALL TOLL FREE
1-800-404-7445
3 LOCATIONS

FT. SMITH
500 W. Code St. Suite 202
JONESVILLE
321 W. Code St. Suite 20
LA CROSSE
232 E. Code St. Suite 110

PHYSICIANS & SURGEONS-M.D.- RHEUMATOLOGY (RHEUMATIC & ARTHRITIC CONDTITIONS)

Arthritis Treatment Center
63 Highway 8 Ft Smith --------------- 866-3242

PHYSICIANS & SURGEONS-M.D.- SPORTS MEDICINE

PETERSON RONALD MD
ORTHOPAEDIC SURGERY SPORTS MEDICINE
ARTHROSCOPY
LIGAMENT RECONSTRUCTION
FRACTURE CARE
26 W. COLUMBUS DR --------- 946-5946

FILLER

FILLER

FILLER

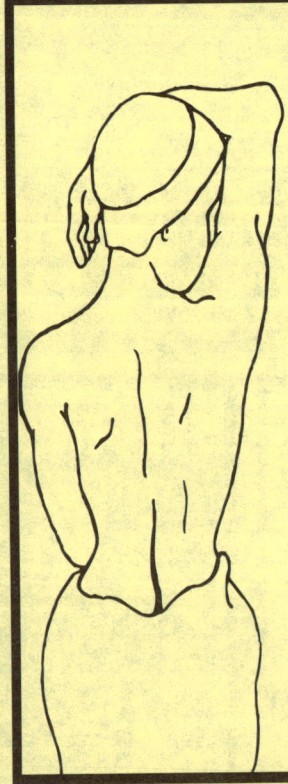

Mammography Screening Education & Intervention

The Breast Center at

Smith County Medical Center

518-8115

Ft Smith Medical Center is conveniently located 1/2 mile east of Hwy 8 on Saxony Avenue

Y-13

PHYSICIANS & SURGEONS-M.D.-SURGERY-COLON & RECTAL

RUSSELL CARL M
Board Certified
Colon & Rental Surgery
Proctology - Colonoscopy

63 S. US HWY 71 & 29 STE 300 -------- 866-1781
6014 W. GOLDEN POND RD
JONESVILLE ----------------------------- 333-2642

Russell Carl M
6014 Golden Pond Rd
Jonesville ------------------------------ 333-2642

PHYSICIANS & SURGEONS-M.D.-SURGERY-GENERAL

CARSON LARRY A MD FICA
General & Vascular Surgery
576 ORCHARD LANE FT SMITH ---------- 637-2623
CLIFFORD DON MD
Peripheral Vascular Surgery
135 S. MARYLAND RD FT SMITH --------- 926-8880
CORBITT TIMOTHY S MD
501 W. POVERTY LANE FT SMITH -------- 837-4111

DONOHUE MARK M MD
DIPLOMATE AMERICAN BOARD
OF SURGERY
GENERAL • VASCULAR
THORACIC SURGERY
448 E. DODGE ST FT SMITH ----------- 837-0035

Dobson & Roberts Surgical Practice
57 Wolf Ridge Ave Ft Smith ------------ 866-3798
PARKER ANTHONY E MD
576 ORCHARD LN FT SMITH ------------ 437-0699
SCHUBERT ROBERT MD
Peripheral Vascular Surgery
135 MARYLAND RD FT SMITH ----------- 926-8880
WONG RICHARD C MD
903 S Maple Ave Jonesville ------------ 223-1677

PHYSICIANS & SURGEONS-M.D.-SURGERY-HAND

Browning Marilyn MD
Morrison Orthopaedic Clinic
6014 Ft Smith Blvd Ft Smith ------------ 333-6383
Toll Free --------------------------- 800-778-5150
FOSTER LEONARD K MD
57 WOLF RIDGE AVE FT SMITH --------- 866-2192

FOSTER AND MASTER MD PA
Diplomate American Board of Surgery
Surgery Of The Hand
Medicare Assignment Accepted
24 hr. Emergency Service

57 WOLF RIDGE AVE FT SMITH --------- 866-2192
166 FT SMITH BLVD FT SMITH ---------- 767-1535

MASTER VICTOR A MD
57 WOLF RIDGE AVE FT SMITH --------- 866-2192

WEST JOSEPHINE B MD
HAND SURGERY
Adult • Pediatric
Orthopaedic Surgery
Member American Society For
Surgery of the Hand

26 E COLUMBUS ST FT SMITH --946-1010

PHYSICIANS & SURGEONS-M.D.-SURGERY-NEUROLOGICAL

McDonnell Miles S MD
7402 State St Jonesville --------------- 987-0058

PHYSICIANS & SURGEONS-M.D.-SURGERY-ORTHOPEDIC

ARNOLD NORMAN J MD
• Adult Reconstructive Surgery
• Arthroscopic Surgery
• Sports Medicine

207 WOLF RIDGE AVE FT SMITH ------- 866-4568
125 E. HWY 334, SUITE 503 JONESVILLE-767-5655
113 S MONARCH RD LA CROSSE -------- 323-3458

Arnold Nolman J MD
113 S. Monarch Rd La Crosse ---------- 323-3458
BOARDMAN TIMOTHY S MD
5651 Stone St Ft. Smith --------------- 987-4646

GALLAGHER MARTIN MD
BOARD CERTIFIED A.B.O.S.
GENERAL ORTHOPAEDICS
& SPINE SURGERY
• Outpatient Laser Surgery • Back & Neck Pain
• Sports Medicine • Fractures • Arthritis
800-393-0308
Se habla Español
FT SMITH ------------------------ 875-0308
South Highway 57 Across From Channel 18
ARLINGTON PLAZA
3293 Arlington St Ft Smith

GIFFORD FRANK M MD
407 E DODGE ST FT SMITH ------------ 437-2219
5651 STONE ST JONESVILLE ----------- 235-0052
HOLLOWAY MARTIN S MD FACS
407 E DODGE ST FT SMITH ------------ 437-2219
5651 STONE ST JONESVILLE ----------- 235-0052
HOWARD RONALD C MD FACS
407 E DODGE ST FT SMITH ------------ 437-2219
5651 STONE ST JONESVILLE ----------- 235-0052
HUBBARD RONALD K MD FACS
407 E DODGE ST FT SMITH ------------ 437-2219
5651 STONE ST JONESVILLE ----------- 235-0052

JUDSON ORTHOPAEDIC CLINIC
North Orange Plaza
515 E. Hwy 443 La Crosse --------- 767-0169
(See Our Display Ad On Page 13)

MORRISON ORTHOPAEDIC CLINIC

MOC

MORRISON
ORTHOPAEDIC CLINIC
Ronald H. Kingman, Sr., M.D.
Marilyn Browning M.D.
Richard C. King, M.D.
Martin Beck, M.D.

6014 FT SMITH BOULEVARD,
FT SMITH -------------------------- 333-6383
6032 N. HARBOR DR
LA CROSSE --------------------- 409-753-0052
---------------------------------- 800-778-5150
6 Other Locations in
Smith, Jones and Foster Counties

We Accept Medicare Assignment

ORTHOPAEDIC GROUP OF SMITH COUNTY
Diplomates American Board of Orthopaedic Surgery

Ronald K. Hubbard, M.D.
Ronald C. Howard, M.D.
Martin S. Holloway, M.D. FACS

Specializing In...
• Joint Replacement
• Sports Medicine
• Athroscopic Surgery
• Back And Neck Disorders
• Disorders Of The Foot And Ankle
• Arthritic Joint Disorders
• Sprains And Fractures
• Knee Injuries
• Adult And Pediatric Orthopaedic Care

TEAM PHYSICIANS FOR
SMITHTOWN COLLEGE
JONESVILLE AND SMITH
HIGH SCHOOLS

Ft Smith
437-2210
407 E. Dodge St.

Jonesville
235-0052
5651 Stone St
Stone Medical Bldg • Suite 402

Serving: Smith Memorial Hospital and Jonesville Medical Center

---

SMITH ORTHOPAEDIC ASSOCIATION

Timothy S. Boardman, M. D.
Samuel T. Russell, M. D.

Diplomates American Board of Orthopaedic Surgery

Practice Limited to Orthopaedic Surgery
NEW PATIENTS WELCOME
3 Convenient Locations

223-6118	987-4646	767-5355
La Crosse Professional Center 108 W 3rd Avenue • La Crosse	Stone Medical Center Suite 105 5651 Stone St • Ft Smith	Jonesville Medical Center 125 E Hwy 443 • Jonesville

---

Judson Orthopaedic Clinic, PA

ESTABLISHED 1956

Diplomates American Academy of
Orthopaedic Surgeons
American Board Of Orthopaedic Surgery

Medicare Assignment Accepted
Subspecialists In
• Total Joint Replacement • Sports Medicine
• Spinal Surgery • Hand & Microvascular Surgery
• General Orthopaedics

Toll Free
1-800-234-5366   **767-0169**
NORTH ORANGE PLAZA
515 E Hwy 443 • Suite 102 • La Crosse

FILLER

FILLER

FILLER

AVENUE PLUMBING INC
"Since 1965"

BRIAN E. AVENUE
3RD GENERATION LICENSED MASTER PLUMBER

SENIOR CITIZENS DISCOUNT

24 HOUR EMERGENCY SERVICE
SAME DAY SERVICE
RESIDENTIAL • COMMERCIAL
Certified Back Flow Prevention/Testing
SOLAR POOL HEATING & REPAIRS
COMPLETE PLUMBING REPAIRS

- Sewer & Drain Cleaning
- Water & Sewer Installations
- Faucets & Garbage Disposals
- Toilets & Toilet Repairs
- Pumps & Pump Repairs • Water Heaters
- Utility Cost. • Lift Station Repairs
- Septic Tanks & Repairs

COMMERCIAL DISCOUNT RATES FOR:
- Restaurants • Churches
- Management/Real Estate
- Condominium Assoc.

JONESVILLE SPECIALISTS IN:
- CEILING AND SLAB LEAKS REPAIRED
- WHOLE HOUSE REPIPING
- WATER & SEWER HOOK-UPS
- DUAL WATER HOOK-UPS
- ☆ NEIGHBORHOOD DISCOUNTS ON SEWER HOOK-UPS

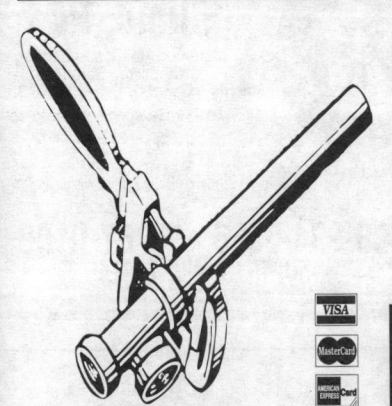

Bonded-Insured

VISA MasterCard AMERICAN EXPRESS DISCOVER

184-1151	245-1244
FT SMITH	JONESVILLE

ROOTER SERVICE OF FT SMITH
PLUMBING SERVICE

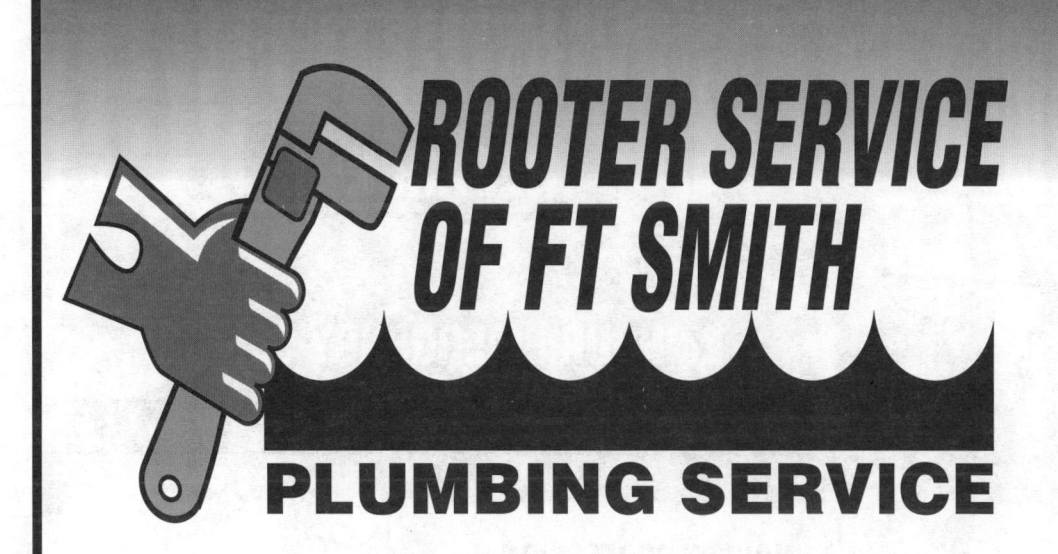

COMPLETE PLUMBING, SEWER & DRAIN CLEANING SERVICE

NO EXTRA CHARGE - NIGHTS/WEEKENDS/HOLIDAYS

SERVICE AVAILABLE 24 HOURS A DAY

ALL TYPES OF PLUMBING REPAIRS

FREE ESTIMATES

SINCE 1950

1 HOUR EMERGENCY SERVICE

VISA MasterCard

SMITH COUNTY
639-7671

JONESVILLE
245-0039

C. HAMMER PLUMBING

REPAIR KIT

COMMERCIAL & RESIDENTIAL

24 HOUR EMERGENCY SERVICE

HONEST PROFESSIONAL SERVICE

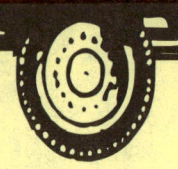

Serving Ft. Smith Area Since 1961

OVER 30 YEARS OF EXPERIENCE   **3RD GENERATION PLUMBING CONTRACTOR**

COMPLETE PLUMBING SALES & SERVICE

- SOLAR SYSTEMS
- WATER FILTERS & CONDITIONERS
- SEWER INSTALLATION
- SEWER & DRAIN CLEANING
- KITCHEN & BATH REMODELING
- WATER SERVICES
- BACKFLOW DEVICE INSTALLATIONS & TESTING

FT. SMITH	S. FT. SMITH	JONESVILLE
693-6757	**814-9126**	**452-6757**

VISA   MasterCard

402-1 CENTER ST. • FT. SMITH

Licensed & Insured

Y-17

PLUMBING CONTRACTORS (CONT.)

AFFORDABLE PLUMBING
QUALITY & PROFESSIONAL WORKMANSHIP
- Repairs & Remodel
- Drain Cleaning
- Dual & City Water Hook Ups
- Water Heaters

Lic. # CPC 1000401

277-1331

---------------------------------------277-1331

ALCOA PLUMBING
CFC3064760
---------------------------------------787-8989

ALL AMERICAN LEAK DETECTION
Electronic Leak Detection Under Concrete Slabs, In Pool Spas, Fountains, And Any Hidden Areas
Lic. # CFC255074

TOLL FREE --------------------------800-396-1673

AMERICAN PLUMBING SERVICE
QUALITY SERVICE
SEWER & WATER HOOK-UPS
WATER HEATERS
REPAIRS/REMODELING
NEW CONSTRUCTION
15 Years Experience
Master Plumber
State Certified RF854037

---------------------------------------523-8500

ANDERSON ROOTER SERVICE

Anderson Rooter Service

**24 HOUR SERVICE
7 DAYS A WEEK**

- WATER HEATERS
- FAUCETS, SINKS
- GARBAGE DISPOSALS
- TOILETS, SEWERS, DRAINS
- ALL REPAIRS

"Serving All Of Smith County"

JONESVILLE-------------------------438-1766
---------------------------------------693-6828

Anderson Rooter Service
---------------------------------------438-1766
A-L PLUMBING
708 NW 74TH AVE ------------------522-1563
ARC PLUMBING COMPANY
1630 SW 2ND ST---------------------277-3389
Artistic Plumbing Service
8003 Date Ave ---------------------432-7003

FILLER

Farragut Plumbing

Fast Dependable Repairs and Drain Cleaning

**Serving Smith County
Reasonable Rates**

572-8723

*"Day or night --
We make it right"*

465 Commercial Blvd.
RESIDENTIAL & COMMERCIAL

14 radio dispatched trucks to serve you

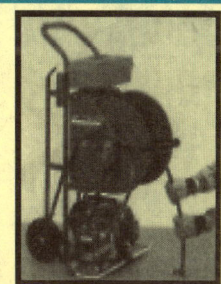

24-Hour Emergency Service
- Maintenance Contracts Available
- Water Heaters
- Clogged Drains
- Leaks & Drips
- Garbage Disposals
- Pump Repairs
- Remodeling
- New Fixtures
- New Construction

Most Parts in Stock VISA MasterCard

Avenue Plumbing
 Smith --------------------------------184-1151
 Jonesville----------------------------245-1244
 (See Our Display Ad On Page 14)
Aztec Plumbing Company
 2192 NW 74th Ave -----------------222-8454
 (See Our Display Ad On Page 21)
B&A PLUMBING
 2380 Dale Ave ---------------------373-1174
 (See Our Display Ad On Page 25)
B & D Plumbing
 33 Pine Road ----------------------599-6281
B & J CONTRACTORS
 1027 QUEEN ST -------------------323-4466
B & N PLUMBING
 --------------------------------------475-1431
BR Plumbing
 562 Gregory St --------------------984-3460
Beeler Plumbing
 5053 North Ave -------------------233-4555
BEST PLUMBING
 (See Ad In Jonesville Directory)
 --------------------------------------745-5665
Bookout Plumbing Service
 2113 Date Ave --------------------373-9921
Burton C. Inc.
 --------------------------------------727-6158
Buxton H G Plumbing
 22210 Huffmaster Rd -------------354-6161

C Hammer Plumbing Service
 402 Center St ---------------------693-6757
 South Ft Smith 402 Center St ----814-9126
 Jonesville-------------------------452-6757
 (See Our Display Ads In Pages 16 & 21)
CAMPBELL PLUMBING
 4011 NW 21st St -----------------277-0074
Carefree Appliances
 625 NW 43rd St ------------------945-3330

DISPLAY FILLER

FILLER

CONWAY PLUMBING
RESIDENTIAL & COMMERCIAL

ON-CALL 24-HOUR EMERGENCY SERVICE

- Faucets
- Drains Cleaned
- Water Treatment
- Garbage Disposals
- Repipes
- Water Heaters
- Pumps
- Sewers
- Fixtures

REPAIRS & REMODELING

DELTA MOEN KOHLER GOULDS

LICENSED & INSURED

FT SMITH
399-0571

LA CROSSE
863-1611

VISA MasterCard

LIBERTY
476-0800

DISPLAY FILLER

PLUMBING CONTRACTORS (CONT)

CHARLIE BLACK'S PLUMBING

Charlie Black's PLUMBING

"Over 25 Years In Ft. Myers"
Residential • Commercial
• Remodeling
"Serving All Of Lee County"
• *Master Plumber License #FC7359300*
• New Installation
• Service & Repair
• Replacements
• Water Heaters

Visa - MasterCard
"Free Estimates"
496-7851
621 Unity St

Chick's Plumbing Service -------- 827-3932
City Plumbing
18117 Hwy 8 -------- 827-2762
COASTLINE PLUMBING SERVICE
-------- 527-8723
(See Our Display Ad On Page 3)
Cohan's Plumbing
7562 Liberation Blvd -------- 233-2895
Connors Plumbing & Mechanical Services Corporation
17782 Oak St. -------- 762-2066
Conway Plumbing
Ft Smith -------- 339-0571
LaCrosse -------- 863-1611
Conway Plumbing
-------- 339-0571
D&M Plumbing
-------- 814-0401
D N King Plumbing
-------- 284-3252
Dad's Plumbing Inc.
12904 Esther Rd -------- 345-6601
DANIEL'S PLUMBING CO.
3052 HIGH ST -------- 433-7921
(See Our Display Ad On Page 23)
Davis Sewer Cleaning
-------- 277-2882

DAWES PLUMBING INC.

Repair & Remodeling
24 HOUR SERVICE
OVER 30 YEARS EXPERIENCE
-------- 345-2222

DEAN'S PLUMBING INC.
Ft Smith -------- 345-2222
-------- 399-0222
Jonesville 3393 Date St -------- 245-3300
Diamond Services
-------- 399-9291
DOVER PLUMBING
16515 N. STONE DR -------- 334-0905
EARLY PLUMBING SERVICE

RESIDENTIAL • MOBILE HOMES
• REPAIRS   • ELECTRIC
• FIXTURE SALES • SEWER CLEANING
Water Heater & Garbage Disposal
Lic RF0000222002
869 BIG POND RD -------- 599-6464

Eagle Rooter
-------- 233-5722

FILLER

Y-19

PLUMBING CONTRACTORS (CONT)

FAITH PLUMBING

Same Day Service
Customer Satisfaction Guaranteed.
Over 23 Years Experience In Fort Smith
All Plumbing Repairs
• Including •
Whole House Repiping
Non-Destructive Leak Detection
Faith Plumbing
639-2888
RF274420
206 MIDDLE AVE ---------------------- 639-2888

Faith Plumbing
  206 Middle Ave ---------------------- 639-2888
  206 Middle Ave ---------------------- 639-4440
FT SMITH PLUMBING
  8372 Brent Ave ---------------------- 233-6363
FORD PLUMBING

FORD PLUMBING
"Your Complete Plumbing Specialist"
Residential/Commercial
Sales
• Briggs • AM Standard • Moen
• Kohler • Ruud • Rheem
• Sta-Rite And More
Service
• Trenching • Elec-Drain Cleaning
• Water Heaters • Water Pumps
• Remodeling • New Construction
• Water Conditioning
Lic#FC006751
Jonesville 475-9691
496-9691
8473 BEACH RD ---------------------- 496-9691

Frank's Plumbing Co.
  10 North Commercial Park ---------------------- 334-1481
France Plumbing Inc.
  Ft Smith ---------------------- 733-6627
France Plumbing Inc.
  709 Golf Rd ---------------------- 475-4121
  (See Our Display Ad On This Page)
Fuller Plumbing Service
  2008 4th Ave NE ---------------------- 963-0886

Gaines Plumbing
  3121 Flower Dr ---------------------- 274-1392
Good Robert Plumbing
  6315 Robin Rd ---------------------- 382-4158
Harm's Plumbing
  Ft Smith ---------------------- 496-4300
  18707 Elm Creek Dr ---------------------- 827-3003
GORDON PLUMBING COMPANY

Gordon Plumbing Company
RESIDENTIAL • COMMERCIAL
"In Business Since 1976"
NEW INSTALLATIONS
REPAIRS
Licensed Bonded & Insured
To Meet All Requirements
State Certified FC0023663
"WEEKEND SERVICE AVAILABLE"

475-1872

7201 NW 21ST ST ---------------------- 475-1872

Hirsch Plumbing Inc.
  12942 Golden Dr ---------------------- 749-055
ITALIAN MECHANICAL
FC0008934 ---------------------- 496-8652

JAMES ROWE PLUMBING
  Ft Smith ---------------------- 762-6231
Jeff Meyers Plumbing & Repairs
   ---------------------- 496-3407
  (See Our Display Ad On Page 25)
Joe Jones Plumbing
  Ft Smith ---------------------- 639-9265
  7034 NE 3rd St ---------------------- 245-4043
Joseph's Plumbing
   ---------------------- 382-8887

FILLER

Kayo Plumbing
  203 Woodlawn St ---------------------- 863-5143
  203 Woodlawn St ---------------------- 963-5143
KING PLUMBING INC.
  11021 AMES LANE ---------------------- 639-7721
Lance's Plumbing
  8123 SE 5th St ---------------------- 475-1516
Larry's Plumbing
  8168 Park South ---------------------- 639-9964
Lawson Contracting Inc.
  1602 Elm St ---------------------- 364-5332
M & C Enterprises of Smith County Inc.
  14781 Richland Rd ---------------------- 317-8200
Master Plumbing Service
  1011 SW Maple St ---------------------- 277-0027
Masterson Plumbing Inc.
  1487 Rosewood Dr ---------------------- 984-0102
McRoberts Thomas G
  3161 Rita St ---------------------- 639-7468
Meager Construction
  4422 NW 62nd Ave ---------------------- 475-0304

SINCE 1971
FRANCE PLUMBING INC

24 Hour Emergency Service

Serving All Smith County For Over 25 Years

SERVICES: • All Plumbing Repairs & Installations • Bath & Kitchen Remodeling
• Water Heaters & Repairs • Electric Sewer & Drain Cleaning • Water Filters
• Insta Hots • Disposals • Fixtures & Parts - All Major Brands • Shower Pans
• Water Saver Products • Sewer, Dual Water & Water Hook-ups
• Repipe Systems • Handicapped Fixtures

SAVE: • No Trip Charge • 1 Year Warranty on all Work • Extended Hours
• SR. Discount on Repairs • Fast Efficient Service - Radio Dispatched
• Mannabloc Repipe - 10 yr. Warranty • Same Day Service (call before 1 p.m.)
• Fully Licensed & Insured

SERVICE • COMMERCIAL • REMODELING • RESIDENTIAL
WE GUARANTEE
CUSTOMER SATISFACTION

JONESVILLE
475-4121

Showroom Counter Sale
907 Golf Road
Jonesville
LIC # FC1967300

FT SMITH
733-6627

FILLER

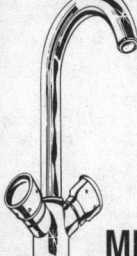

NATION'S BEST PLUMBER

MECHANICAL CONTRACTORS
PLUMBING SERVICE DIVISION

FULL SERVICE PLUMBER

RESIDENTIAL & COMMERCIAL

☑ **NO OVERTIME CHARGE**
☑ **NO TRIP OR TRAVEL TIME CHARGE**

- All Types of Plumbing
- Water Heaters
- Sewer & Drain
- Repairs - Service - Remodeling

LICENSED INSURED
#RF167290

"All Work Guaranteed"

24 HOUR EMERGENCY SERVICE
7 DAYS A WEEK

FREE ESTIMATES

475-9323

TOLL-FREE 1-800-475-3503

VISA • MasterCard • American Express • Discover

PLUMBING CONTRACTORS (CONT)

METROPOLITAN PLUMBING SERVICE
1426 Metropolitan Rd Ft Smith --------- 572-5235
MICKEY'S PLUMBING
-- 284-3252
Mike's Plumbing Service
-- 863-6056
Nation's Best Plumber
5192 NE 3rd Av --------------------------- 475-9323
Nice Plumbing Service
15706 Slate St ---------------------------- 433-1824
North Ft Smith Plumbing
-- 599-6756
Palmer Plumbing Co
2072 Gregory Ave ------------------------ 433-1824
(See Our Display Ad On Page 24)
Panel Plumbing Co
Ft Smith ---------------------------------- 334-3430
Jonesville ------------------------------- 245-4029
(See Our Display Ad On Page 22)
Partner's Plumbing Inc.
-- 762-3802
(See Our Display Ad On Page 3)

PECAN PLUMBING CO

Residential • Commercial Remodeling

- All Plumbing Repairs & Installations
- Remodeling - Baths & Kitchens. Electric Sewer & Drain Cleaning
- Water Heaters - Repair & Installations
- Water & Sewer Hook-up Installations

Installations of Water Purification Systems

Free Estimates
State Lic RF052494

5465 YOUNGSTOWN RD ---------------- 984-9393

PERFECT PLUMBING CO
- Sewer & Drain Cleaning
- Complete Plumbing Service
- Water Heaters • Remodeling
"SENIOR CITIZEN DISCOUNT"
State Certified Lic. # RF808954

-- 762-5650

Plumbing By Tom
838 NW 8th Ave -------------------------- 277-3834
QUALIFIED PLUMBING
145 NW 23RD AV ------------------------- 277-4468

R J'S PLUMBING INC.
SPECIALIZING IN:
- *COMMERCIAL*
- *MULTI-FAMILY*
- *INDUSTRIAL*

State Certified Lic. # RF808954

7092 COMMERCIAL AVE ---------------- 733-1104

R L Williams Plumbing
Ft Smith ---------------------------------- 233-0445
7552 Orange St --------------------------- 656-3500
(See Our Display Ad On Page 22)

DISPLAY FILLER

FILLER

Y-21

AZTEC PLUMBING COMPANY

Specializing In Repairs & Remodeling

"Building a Reputation Based Upon Quality Service"

Quality Service at Competitive Prices

All Work Guaranteed

- ✓ Water and Sewer Hook-Ups
- ✓ Water Heaters (All Brands)
- ✓ Re-Piping
- ✓ Sewer & Drain Cleaning
- ✓ Tubs, Toilets, Sinks
- ✓ Complete Line of Plumbing Fixtures

FREE ESTIMATES
COMPARE OUR RATES

JONESVILLE **222-8454**
FT SMITH **639-4691**

2192 NW 74th Ave

24 HOUR Emergency Service

VISA MasterCard

★ ★ ★ ★ ★ ★ ★ ★ ★ ★

C HAMMER PLUMBING SERVICE

COMMERCIAL & RESIDENTIAL
24 HOUR EMERGENCY SERVICE
NEW CONSTRUCTION & REPAIRS

693-6757   814-9126   452-6757

VISA MasterCard

(402 Center St • Ft Smith)

PANEL PLUMBING CO

State Certified # RF77692

WEEKEND AND EARLY EVENING APPOINTMENTS ACCEPTED

THE REPAIR & REMODEL SPECIALIST

Residential - Commercial
Over 30 Years Experience

- Water Heaters
- Water Pumps
- Water Purification
- Mobile Homes
- Faucets
- Garbage Disposals
- Drain Cleaning
- Hydro Jetting
- Fixtures
- Backflow Testing
- Remodeling
- Re-piping

24 HOUR EMERGENCY SERVICE

JONESVILLE
245-4029
8131 NW 1st. St.

FT SMITH
334-3430
8075 Youngstown Road

VISA — DISCOVER — Mastercard

RL WILLIAMS PLUMBING

SAME DAY SERVICE

24 Hour Service - No Overtime Charge
(Nights, Weekends, Holidays No Extra Charge)

ALL WORK GUARANTEED
Residential & Commercial

SEE OUR OFFER IN THE COUPON SECTION

WE SPECIALIZE IN WATER & SEWER REPIPES

- Water Heaters • Water Pumps • Electric Sewer & Drain Cleaning
- Lift Station Repairs • Sewer & Water Installations • Backflow Testing & Repairs

FREE ESTIMATES

State Certified # RF807530

FT SMITH
233-0445

NORTH FT SMITH
656-3500

LICENSED
BONDED
INSURED

Y-23

UNITED SERVICES INC

SINCE 1969 — "Service You Can Depend On"

24 HOURS/7 DAYS — ALWAYS PROMPT & RELIABLE

COMPLETE PLUMBING SALES & SERVICE

- Re-piping
- Faucets - Toilets - Sinks - Tubs
- Water Heaters - Water Pumps - Garbage Disposals
- Water Purification - Softeners - Filters
- Sewer & Water Line Installation
- Sewer & Drain Electrically Cleaned
- Core Drilling - Trenching
- Backflow Preventer Installation & Testing

FT SMITH 284-8883
5925 Youngstown Rd
(LIC CFC0696930)

JONESVILLE 245-2252

VISA MasterCard

The grace of the past and the promise of the future.

THE HERITAGE SUITE

The Heritage suite, A luxury suite of flawlessly designed bathroom fixtures. A perfect union of timeless lines and modern innovation created by American Standard.

Luxury

Bath Gallery Showroom

American Standard
Living up to a higher standard

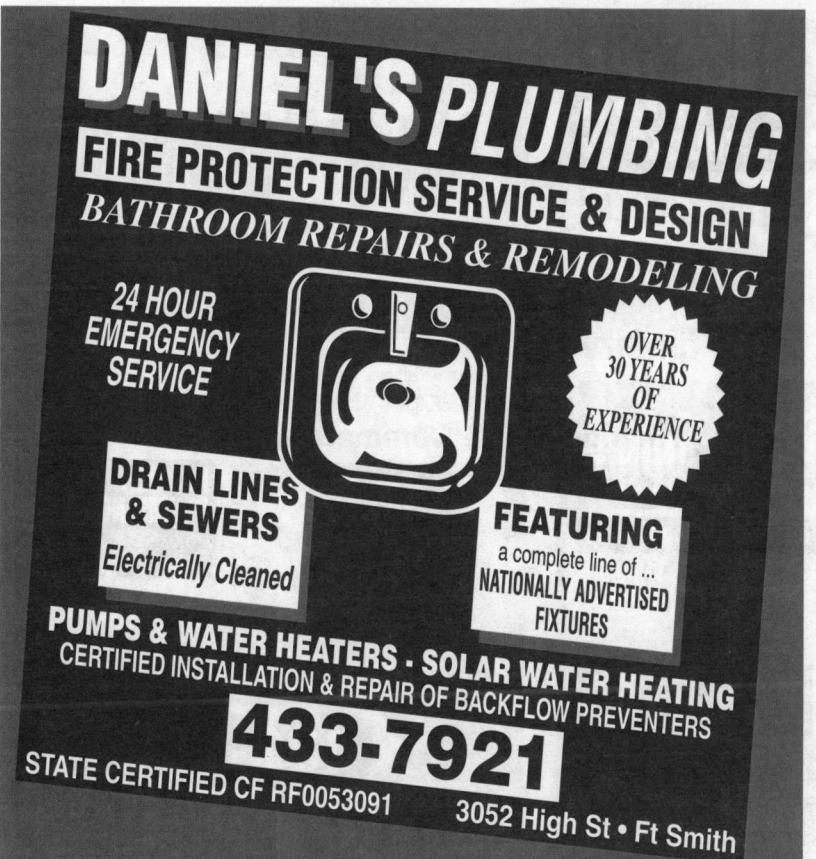

284-7154

DANIEL'S PLUMBING
FIRE PROTECTION SERVICE & DESIGN
BATHROOM REPAIRS & REMODELING

24 HOUR EMERGENCY SERVICE

OVER 30 YEARS OF EXPERIENCE

DRAIN LINES & SEWERS Electrically Cleaned

FEATURING a complete line of ... NATIONALLY ADVERTISED FIXTURES

PUMPS & WATER HEATERS - SOLAR WATER HEATING
CERTIFIED INSTALLATION & REPAIR OF BACKFLOW PREVENTERS

433-7921

STATE CERTIFIED CF RF0053091   3052 High St • Ft Smith

PLUMBING CONTRACTORS (CONT)

RAYMOND'S PLUMBING
Repair & Remodel Specialists 475-3272

Rex Smith's Plumbing
3006 Easy St 364-5919

Rice Plumbing Service 433-1062

RICHARDS PLUMBING CO
17500 HOMESITE RD 382-6262
MAIN OFFICE 277-4081

RON'S PLUMBING
Residential • Commercial
New Construction
Repair • Remodel
Water Heaters
State Certified Lic. # RF808954
1004 MILITARY RD 496-4696

Ron's Plumbing
2631 Pine Tree Rd 317-5222

ROOTER SERVICE OF FT SMITH
FT SMITH 312-4343
JONESVILLE 345-7676
(See Our Display Ad On Page 15)

S & P PLUMBING CONTRACTORS
State Cert. # to RF054753
Residential & Commercial
11600 COMMERCIAL BLVD 664-0002

SAMPSON PLUMBING CO
Plumbing Repairs
Drain & Sewer Cleaning
24 Hour Emergency Service
Heating Repairs
433-8698
30 Years State Certified
4732 FREEDOM AVE 433-8698

JOE JONES PLUMBING

REPAIR & REMODELING SPECIALIST
RESIDENTIAL • COMMERCIAL

OUR SERVICES...
- All plumbing repairs & installations.
- Remodeling - Baths & Kitchens.
- Electric sewer & drain cleaning
- Water heaters repair & installations.
- Solar heating - repairs & installations.
- Specialists in complete repiping of water lines.

SAVE...
- ALL WORK GUARANTEED 1 YEAR
- FREE ESTIMATES

27 YEARS EXPERIENCE

24 HOUR EMERGENCY SERVICE
EVENING & WEEKEND APPOINTMENTS

STATE CERTIFIED # RF050755

Jonesville **245-4043**
Ft Smith **639-9265**

INSURED

PLUMBING CONTRACTORS (CONT)

Scott Robert H. Plumbing Co
5962 Gregory St. — 233-8473
Scotty Williams Plumbing
608 NW 74th St — 245-8564
Summers Plumbing
7586 Wildwood Ave — 939-2752
Sweetwater Sewer & Plumbing Co
— 274-9234
Thomas Plumbing Co
— 799-7715
TOWN PLUMBING & SEWER SERVICE
8031 HAMPTON ST — 233-1941
(See Our Display Ad On Page 25)
TRI COUNTY PLUMBING CO.
3325 NE 9TH ST — 245-9775
True Pro Plumbing
— 245-7870

FILLER

A ROOTER SERVICE
"RADIO DISPATCHED TRUCKS"

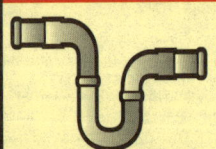

ANY Drain Cleaned

Since 1973

Serving All Of Smith County

Professional DRAIN & SEWER CLEANING

- Hydro Jet Cleaners
- The Latest Equipment For Any Size Line
- Low, Fair Rates
- Residential • Commercial

Minor Plumbing Repairs
- Sewers • Sinks • Drains
- Tubs • Stools • Lavatories
- Septic Tanks

733-3335   **245-0149**

Fast 24 Hour, 7 Day Service
IF WE CAN'T FIX IT, IT AIN'T BROKE
LICENSE # CFC0505983

"Serving Entire Area Since 1964"

PALMER PLUMBING CO

"SPECIALIZING IN REPAIRS & REMODELING"

- Water heaters
- Faucets
- Toilets
- Bath Tubs
- Garbage Disposals
- Sewer Lines Cleaned
- Kitchen & Bathroom Sinks
- Water Pump Systems
- Back Flow Certification Repairs
- Water Purification Systems

Leak Detection & Water Repiping

OVER 30 YEARS OF EXPERIENCE

PALMER PLUMBING CO

24 HOUR EMERGENCY SERVICE
7 DAYS PER WEEK   NIGHTS & WEEKENDS

433-1824

STATE LICENSE # CFC0320963
2072 GREGORY AVE • FT SMITH

PLUMBING CONTRACTORS (CONT)

Union Plumbing
1033 Hansen Ave — 433-5431
United Services Inc
5295 Youngstown Rd — 284-8883
WATER'S PLUMBING, INC.
7221 NW 8TH ST — 323-3434
14264 BEACH SIDE DR — 496-0072

PLUMBING SEWER & DRAIN CLEANING

A ECONOMICAL PLUMBER
FT SMITH — 233-5722
A Rooter Woman
Ft Smith — 733-5333
Affordable Plumbing
— 277-1331
Anderson Rooter Service
Ft Smith — 693-6828
B&A PLUMBING
2380 DALE AVE — 373-1174
B&D PLUMBING
33 PINE RD — 599-6281
France Plumbing Inc.
907 Golf Rd — 475-4121
Palmer Plumbing Co
2072 Gregory Ave — 433-1824

PLUMBING REPAIRS
24 Hour Emergency Service

B&A Plumbing
Serving All Of Smith County Since 1980
AUTHORIZED DEALER FOR RHEEM
Electric Rooter Machine — Water Heaters
Kitchen & Bathroom Remodeling
SAME DAY SERVICE
373-1174
LIC # RF075940
2380 DALE AVE • FT SMITH

FAST EFFICIENT - 24 HOUR SERVICE
C. Burton, Inc.
A Subsidiary of Hall & Burton, Inc.
Established 1929

DUAL WATER HOOK-UPS
HANDI-CAP CONVERSIONS

THREE GENERATIONS OF MASTER PLUMBERS
Residential • Restaurant • Commercial
New Construction & Remodeling
Hot Water Heaters • Drain Cleaning • Repiping • Gas Piping
State Lic. # RF063665
1 Year Warranty - Free Estimates
CORPORATE DISCOUNTS
SENIOR CITIZENS DISCOUNTS
727-6158
NO TRIP CHARGE
NO OVERTIME CHARGE

EARL'S TOWN
PLUMBING & SEWER SERVICE
ESTABLISHED IN 1958
OVER 35 YEARS OF EXPERIENCE
REPAIR & REMODELING
WATER HEATERS - SALES & SERVICE
RESIDENTIAL & COMMERCIAL -
SPECIALIZING IN SERVICE & REPAIR
ELECTRIC SEWER & DRAIN CLEANING
233-1941
SERVING ALL FT SMITH & SMITH COUNTY
LICENSED & BONDED * INSURED TO MEET AREA REQUIREMENTS
RF085320   8552 KATHLEEN AVE

JEFF MEYERS
PLUMBING & REPAIRS
License # RF07140
- Water Pumps • Water Heaters
- High Pressure 3000 PSI Sewer & Drain Cleaning
- Back Flow Prevention • Leaky Pipes

24 HOUR EMERGENCY SERVICE
496-3407

WATER'S PLUMBING CO
24 HR. EMERGENCY SERVICE
SPECIALIZING IN:
- Repiping
- Hidden Leaks
- All Repairs

STATE CERTIFICATION # RF070632
475-6232
VISA   MasterCard
7221 NW 8th ST

PARTNER'S PLUMBING INC
A Full Service Plumber
Drains - Fixtures - Water Heaters - Etc
Prompt, Reliable Service
Residential & Commercial
24 HOUR EMERGENCY
762-3802
NEW REPAIR REMODELING
ST. CERTIFIED RF007530 - Over 15 Years in Smith County

Y-26

PRINTERS

ACE PRESS

ACE PRESS

Smith County's Leading Offset Printer

Large Format, High Quality
5 Color 26"x40"
Brochures, Business Cards
Menus, Packaging, Posters,
Poster Art, Videocassette,
Sleeves, Direct Mail & More

732-4744
Fax 233-8735
3053 Labor Rd, Ft. Smith
La Crosse: 863-2383
3155 7th Ave, NE

See our other ads under:
Screen Printing & Signs

Ace Press
  3155 7th Ave, NE --------------------- 863-8666
Quick Printing Centers
  1011 Flower Dr ---------------------- 274-1212

BOLLAND'S PRINTING

Quality Commercial
Printing
Graphic Design • Layout
Typesetting • Wedding Invitations
Announcements
Mon-Fri 8:30 to 5

6042 MEXICO AVE ------------------ 433-7581

BUDGET QUICK PRINT

BUDGET QUICK PRINT
572-2323

PRINTING • TYPESETTING • COPYING
-Over 30 Years Exp.-
Willing to Work With You On
Design, Concepts & Editorial

Dedicated To Quality And Service
Open 8:30 to 5
Monday-Friday

12579 KENTON RD -------------------- 572-2323

Certified Printers
  ---------------------------------- 284-8810
Christopher Printing
  1616 Davis Road -------------------- 736-8647
Conway Corp
  10915 Carlton Blvd ----------------- 364-2334

FILLER

QUALITY FULL COLOR PRINTING

FREE PICK-UP AND DELIVERY

Second Day Service on Most Orders

FORMULA PRINTING SERVICES

CALL FOR FREE QUOTATION

1453 Fortune Ave Ft Smith (In Columbia Center)

939-1131

FAX Us Your Requirements at 939-3087

Forms • Letterheads • Envelopes • Brochures • Flyers
Business & Appt. Cards • Menus • Posters • Booklets • Newsletters

Attention, BUSINESSPERSON

939-3602

FAX 939-7365

Discover the Color of

MELVIN PRINTING

SAME DAY SERVICE
ORDERS MUST BE PLACED BY NOON.

FREE PICK-UP & DELIVERY

For All Your Printing Needs

- Layout & Design
- Labels
- Rubber Stamps
- Circulars
- Newsletters
- Books
- Pamphlets
- Adv. Specialties
- Business Forms
- Photo Copies - All Sizes
- Envelopes
- Business Cards
- NCR Forms
- Tickets
- Letterheads
- Continuous Forms

1/4 MILE NORTH OF BELL MALL
1073 Indiana St • Ft Smith

Y-27

"Making Our Mark With Service"
Confidentiality and Security Guaranteed
Full Service Printing

- Stationary
- Envelopes
- Business Cards
- Color Copies
- Carbonless Forms
- Wedding Invitations

SPEEDY PRINTING SERVICE

JONESVILLE
8144-A Parade Blvd
945-3433
FAX 945-1159

FT SMITH
6044 Indiana St
639-8383
FAX 639-7059

FT SMITH-FOUNDRY
5433 Foundry Ave
572-7975
FAX 572-5710

N FT SMITH
12304 Indiana St
656-5553
FAX 656-1164

Family Owned and Operated
FREE PICK-UP AND DELIVERY

PRINTERS (CONT.)

CORNER PRINT SHOP

CORNER PRINT SHOP
FLYERS
MINI MENUS
BUSINESS CARDS
CARBONLESS FORMS
RUBBER STAMPS
LOWEST PRICES
ON THE CAPE
549-4343
FOR ALL YOUR PRINTING NEEDS
235 NW 46TH ST --------------- 549-4343

CUMMING'S COPY CENTER
3321 CENTER ST --------------- 733-7681
Curry Fast Print
1563 Dave St --------------- 639-9912
Desktop Center
9865 Invitation Dr --------------- 799-5993

FILLER

DIRECTIONAL PRINTING

Directional Printing
Commercial Printing
Direct Mail Marketing

- **Commercial Printing**
- **In-House 4-Color Printing**
- **Publications**
- **Newsletters**
- **High Volume Orders**
- **In House Bindery**
- **Typesetting**
- **Direct Mail**

945-4844

5331 MYSTIC ST --------------- 945-4844

DISTINCTIVE PRINTING
THE PRINTING PROFESSIONALS
Guaranteed Quality
One to full color on-site-printing
Competitive Prices • Pick-up & Delivery
6212 Allison Ave --------------- 284-2626
Easy Printing
7041 Division Blvd Jonesville --------------- 854-6333
EMPIRE PRINTING
2692 INDIANA ST --------------- 233-5110
Fast Form Service
1471 Colonial St Ft Smith --------------- 939-0053
Foreman Printing & Graphics Services
3084 Canada Ave --------------- 945-6761

QUICK PRINTING CENTER

"RUSH ORDERS DON'T UPSET US"

BELL MALL
4324 Indiana St
639-1142 • FAX **639-6692**

DOWNTOWN
1022 Second Ave
233-8791 • FAX **233-6521**

HARVEY
16775 Spaulding Blvd
284-0087 • FAX **284-8407**

JONESVILLE
1042 Visitor Blvd
277-0060 • FAX **277-1361**

UNIVERSITY DR
1736 Congressional Dr
334-0013 • FAX **334-3080**

FREE ESTIMATES
PICK-UP - DELIVERY

SPECIAL LASER GRAPHICS

COLOR
IT'S OUR ONLY BUSINESS

HIGH QUALITY FULL COLOR LASER PRINTING FEATURING THE CANON "CLC500" COLOR LASER COPIER

COLOR OUTPUT FROM YOUR COMPUTER DISKS

- Copies From Photos/Original Art/Slides/Negatives/Film Transparencies
- Reductions/Enlargements (50%-400%)
- Wall Graphics & Signage
- Antique Photo Reproduction
- Photo Retouching
- Complete Page Layout & Scanning
- Brochures/Sell Sheets/Pamphlets
- Overhead Transparencies

334-0550

5968 University Blvd - Rembrandt Center

PRINTERS (CONT.)

FORMULA PRINTING SERVICES
1453 Fortune Ave ---------- 939-1131
(See Our Display Ad On Page 26)

GOPHER PRESS PRINTING
991 NW 14TH ST ---------- 277-0026

Graphic Printers & Lithographers
5835 Jasper Rd ---------- 233-6033

House of Printing of Ft Smith
11654 US Hwy 8 ---------- 964-0261

INSTANT PRINTERS
- IN HOUSE THERMOGRAPHY
- MULTI-COLOR PRINTING
- TYPESETTING • BUSINESS CARDS
- NEWSLETTERS • INVOICES
- LETTERHEADS • ENVELOPES
- FAX SERVICE
- DELIVERY AVAILABLE

639-0055
FAX ---------- 639-5655
11258 S INDIANA ST ---------- 639-0055

Inland Graphics Printing & Design
954 Flower Ave ---------- 274-7344

Inland Press Printing
See our ad under Copying Service
15155 Cottonwood Dr Ft Smith ---------- 664-8866

Kaleidoscope Printing Co
208 SW 42nd St ---------- 277-1718

King of Copy
14108 S Indiana St ---------- 939-0045

KING PRINTING & COPIES
15711 INDIANA ST ---------- 639-6677
(See Our Display Ad On This Page)

Kostner Printing Inc.
7491 Sunrise Rd ---------- 433-0207

Kwik Printing & Copy
2026 Congretional Rd ---------- 334-1132

Larsen Print Shop
4041 Jonesville Parkway ---------- 245-2363

LONGFELLOW & TYLER PRINTING
6102 JAMES ST ---------- 433-7178

Magic Printing & Copying
5012 E Second Ave ---------- 233-6544
Fax ---------- 733-3880

Magic Printing Co
6154 Golf Club Rd ---------- 549-5113

Masterful Printing Press
15031 Urban Rd ---------- 772-1839

Morrison Business Forms Inc.
808 NW 48th St ---------- 733-9111

New Jersey Printing
2243 Rodent Ave ---------- 733-9914

New Printing & Copying Center
5425 Lewis Rd ---------- 572-5576

Open & Shut Book Printing
16596 Spalding Ave ---------- 664-6261

PRINT PORS
- Full Service Printing
- Layout & Typesetting
- All Computer Forms, Custom or Stock
- *Customers Rate Us TOPS*
- *Free Pick-Up & Delivery*
- Downtown - Between Fuller and U.S. 8

6032 LIBERATION BLVD. ---------- 233 0068

KING PRINTING & COPIES
Ft Smith
15711 Indiana St
MON-FRI 8AM-5PM
VISA • MasterCard

QUALITY COPIES
- Volume Copy Discounts
- Color Laser Copies

DESKTOP PUBLISHING
- Hourly Macintosh/IBM Rentals
- High Resolution/Color Output

FINISHING SERVICES
- Collating & Binding
- Cutting & Folding

OPEN 24 HOURS

FREE PICK-UP & DELIVERY

639-6677
FAX 572-4646

PRINTING HOUSE
5034 Fuller St (Corner of Fuller and Main) Ft Smith

Professional Printing • Business Promotions
Copy Service • Typesetting/Layout • FAX Service

QUALITY PRINTING • DEPENDABLE SERVICE
COMPETITIVE PRICES

HOURS: Monday thru Friday
9 a.m. to 5:30 p.m.

639-2102

Seriously Speedy Printing

FAX • GRAPHIC DESIGN • TYPESETTING • PRINTING • COPYING • BINDERY

Letterheads • Envelopes • Business Cards • Brochures • Booklets • Directories
Carbonless Forms • Continuous Forms • Snap-apart Forms • Hi-Speed Copying • Invitations
Electronic Publishing on CD-ROM

6412 Spaulding Blvd
King Plaza
233-6460
FAX 233-5301

11320 Urban Blvd
1 Block N. of Main
939-9995
FAX 939-8601

Printer's Alley
Quality Commercial Printing

Business Forms
Color Brochures
Financial Printing
Presentation Folders
Newsletters/Publications
Typesetting & Design

433-8111
3312 Boardwalk • Ft. Smith

Kwik Printing & Copy

Located in N. Ft Smith off University
2026 Congressional Rd
334-1132

Commercial Printing • High Speed Copying
Design Consultation • Desktop Publishing

"When it has to be RIGHT and it has to be NOW!"

The following three pages illustrate even more combinations of layouts, copy content, and color to give you side-by-side comparisons of different ad features. Each layout and design speaks for itself. The following are my comments about each of the layouts on pages Y-30 and Y-31. Comments for the ads on page Y-32 appear on that page.

Layout #1 This plain, black ad is used as a starting point only. There is no reason for an ad to look like this. The buyer of such an ad simply is not putting his or her advertising money to work as hard as it is capable of working.

Layout #2 While the addition of color does help this ad somewhat, it still is much weaker than it has to be for the money that is being spent for such an ad.

Layout #3 The addition of some simple artwork improves the image of the ad. It contains the same message as Layout #1 but presents it more effectively.

Layout #4 The addition of color to the layout again improves the eye appeal of the ad, which should produce additional calls from the ad.

Layout #5 The ad has been improved by the addition of more information for the potential customers of this business. This ad will produce more calls than any of the examples on page 30 even though the two with color would cost the advertiser more than this ad.

Layout #6 The ad again demonstrates the use of a single color to increase the pulling power of the ad. The use of one additional color is the most economical way to utilize color in an ad.

Layout #7 The ad uses red, green, and blue ink in addition to black. This process is called spot color. It costs more than using one additional color and must be used effectively to merit the additional cost.

Layout #8 The ad uses process color. The range of colors available in the process goes way beyond spot color. This process is not available in all directories; however its availability is increasing, especially with many of the larger publishers in the Yellow Pages industry.

These two pages should give you a good feel for the fine points of improving the eye appeal of an ad and its selling message as well. Content is of extreme importance in the results produced by an ad. Yellow Pages users (like yourself) are usually looking for information to help them decide where to buy the product or service they need or want. In the final analysis, I would not run any of the ads on page Y-30 for this business. Certainly some of them are better than others, but none of them would be as effective as the ads on page Y-31.

The differences in the ads on page Y-31 are not in content but rather in the use or non-use of color. Everything has its price. If you believe the ad with one color is better than the ad with no color, then you understand why color costs more. If you believe the last two ads are better yet, then you understand why they would cost even more.

T. G. D.
Auto Air Conditioning & Electric Service

- Climate Control
- Manual A/C Systems
- Complete Auto Repair

Fast Courteous Service
Long Convenient Hours
Open 6 Days
Monday-Saturday 7:30 AM - 7:30 PM

647-3990

101 MARINER WAY

Layout #1

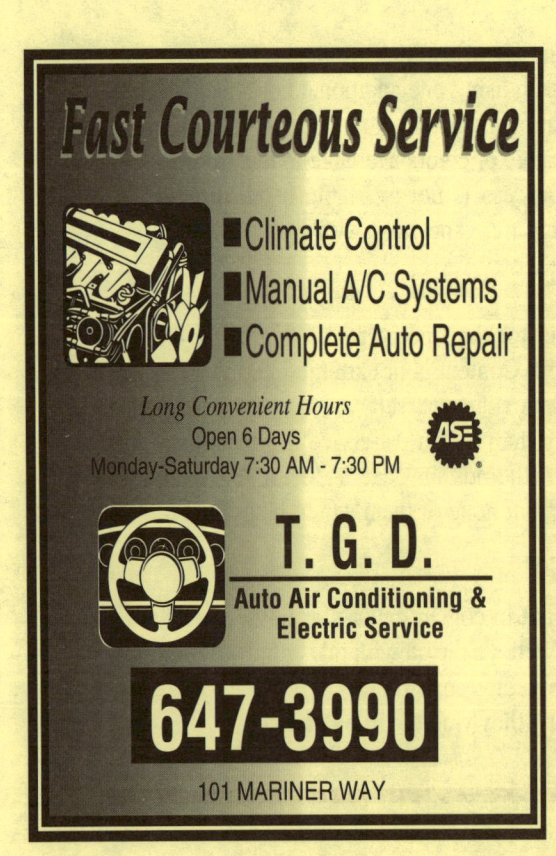

T. G. D.
Auto Air Conditioning & Electric Service

- Climate Control
- Manual A/C Systems
- Complete Auto Repair

Fast Courteous Service
Long Convenient Hours
Open 6 Days
Monday-Saturday 7:30 AM - 7:30 PM

647-3990

101 MARINER WAY

Layout #2

Fast Courteous Service

- Climate Control
- Manual A/C Systems
- Complete Auto Repair

Long Convenient Hours
Open 6 Days
Monday-Saturday 7:30 AM - 7:30 PM

ASE

T. G. D.
Auto Air Conditioning & Electric Service

647-3990

101 MARINER WAY

Layout #3

Fast Courteous Service

- Climate Control
- Manual A/C Systems
- Complete Auto Repair

Long Convenient Hours
Open 6 Days
Monday-Saturday 7:30 AM - 7:30 PM

ASE

T. G. D.
Auto Air Conditioning & Electric Service

647-3990

101 MARINER WAY

Layout #4

Layout #5

Layout #6

Layout #7

Layout #8

Y-32

AFFORDABLE PLUMBING
QUALITY & PROFESSIONAL WORKMANSHIP
- Repairs & Remodel
- Drain Cleaning
- Dual & City Water Hook Ups
- Water Heaters

Lic. # CPC 1000401

277-1331
---------------------------------277-1331

AFFORDABLE PLUMBING
QUALITY & PROFESSIONAL WORKMANSHIP
- Repairs & Remodel
- Drain Cleaning
- Dual & City Water Hook Ups
- Water Heaters

Lic. # CPC 1000401

277-1331
---------------------------------277-1331

AFFORDABLE PLUMBING
QUALITY & PROFESSIONAL WORKMANSHIP
- Repairs & Remodel
- Faucets • Sinks • Toilets & Disposals
- Dual & City Water Hook Ups
- Water Heaters • Drain Cleaning
- Commercial & Residential
- Free Estimates • All Work Guaranteed

Lic. # CPC 1000401

277-1331
---------------------------------277-1331

AFFORDABLE PLUMBING
QUALITY & PROFESSIONAL WORKMANSHIP
- Repairs & Remodel
- Faucets • Sinks • Toilets & Disposals
- Dual & City Water Hook Ups
- Water Heaters • Drain Cleaning
- Commercial & Residential
- Free Estimates • All Work Guaranteed

Lic. # CPC 1000401

277-1331
---------------------------------277-1331

In the above examples, I have taken an existing three-inch ad from the PLUMBING CONTRACTORS heading in The Yellow Pages Sampler. The first example on the left is as the ad appears on page Y-17. In the second example, you can see the effect of adding some simple artwork to help draw attention to the ad. In the third example, the message has been expanded to appeal to a greater percentage of the readers of this ad. Finally, in the fourth example, you can see how effective use of color and illustration improves the ad's ability to attract attention. Spending the additional dollars to buy color effectively for in-column ads can be a good decision because of the relatively low total cost to add color to such ads.

DEAN BROTHERS, INC.
Free Delivery Available
- Cedar Cypress
- Smooth & Rough Treatment
- Fence Poles & Posts

Building Materials
- Painted & Galvanized Steel
- Roofing • Siding Accessories
- Wire • Smooth • Barbed • Bench

Custom Cut Lumber
Serving Lee County Since 1932

688-1413

102 W. 4th Ave. • Ft Smith

DEAN BROTHERS, INC.
Free Delivery Available
- Cedar Cypress
- Smooth & Rough Treatment
- Fence Poles & Posts

Building Materials
- Painted & Galvanized Steel
- Roofing • Siding Accessories
- Wire • Smooth • Barbed • Bench

Custom Cut Lumber
Serving Lee County Since 1932

688-1413

102 W. 4th Ave. • Ft Smith

Free Delivery Available
Building Materials

DEAN BROTHERS INC.
- Cedar Cypress
- Smooth & Rough Treatment
- Fence Poles & Posts

- Painted & Galvanized Steel
- Roofing • Siding Accessories
- Wire • Smooth • Barbed • Bench

Custom Cut Lumber
Serving Lee County Since 1932

688-1413

102 W. 4th Ave. • Ft Smith

Free Delivery Available
Building Materials

DEAN BROTHERS INC.
- Cedar Cypress
- Smooth & Rough Treatment
- Fence Poles & Posts

- Painted & Galvanized Steel
- Roofing • Siding Accessories
- Wire • Smooth • Barbed • Bench

Custom Cut Lumber
Serving Lee County Since 1932

688-1413

102 W. 4th Ave. • Ft Smith

The above examples again show how a basic, simple layout can be improved upon with a little bit of creativity. The first ad on the left is used as the sample to be improved. The second example demonstrates how additional eye appeal can be achieved merely by adding a stronger border. The third example uses the same copy content, but the layout has been totally changed to add even more eye appeal. In most directories it costs no more to purchase the second and third ads above than it does the first example. Finally, the fourth example again shows how effective use of color can increase the attention-getting quality of an ad. Of all of the display ad sizes this is the most economical one to consider adding color to.